DALLAS

DALLAS

A History of "Big D"

By Michael V. Hazel

TEXAS STATE
HISTORICAL ASSOCIATION

Library of Congress Cataloging-in-Publication Data

Hazel, Michael V., 1948–
   Dallas : a history of "Big D" / by Michael V. Hazel
     p.   cm.   —(Fred Rider Cotten popular history series ; no. 11)
   Includes bibliographical references.
   ISBN 0-87611-163-0 (alk. paper)
   1. Dallas (Tex.)—History. I. Texas State Historical Association. II. University of
   Texas at Austin. Center for Studies in Texas History. III. Title. IV. Series
   F394.D2157H28   1997
   976.4'2811—dc21   94-30886
                                                  CIP

Published by the Texas State Historical Association in cooperation with the Center
for Studies in Texas History at the University of Texas at Austin.

Cover: Dallas skyline at sunset, reflected in the Trinity River. Photograph by James
F. Wilson.

CONTENTS

1.
ESTABLISHING A TOWN

THE HISTORY OF DALLAS as a permanent settlement begins in 1841, when the first Anglo pioneers arrived. Native Americans certainly traversed this area on hunting expeditions for thousands of years before then, but there is little evidence of prolonged encampment. Traces of conical structures typical of Caddo farm sites have been found in the Mountain Creek drainage area southwest of Dallas, and prehistoric tools and spear points have been unearthed on the edge of downtown Dallas. But such artifacts are still very rare, and knowledge about these early inhabitants of the region is scanty. In general, the Trinity River, which cuts the modern city in half, seems to have been a sort of dividing line between the more agrarian tribes of eastern Texas and the nomadic, buffalo hunting tribes of the west.[1]

The primary asset of most of what is now Dallas County was its rich, blackland soil. "It is universally admitted to be the finest soil in the country," wrote Edward Smith, an Englishman who visited the region shortly after Texas joined the Union, "equalling in fertility the rich alluvial bottoms of the great Mississippi valley."[2] Apparently his description was not too exaggerated, for an early settler wrote as follows: "This portion of the country is just as rich as any man wants it to be. The soil is black and sticky as far and deep as necessary. Corn, wheat and cotton grow well...."[3]

Certainly this rich soil featured prominently in the advertisements of the Texan Land and Emigration Company, a group of Louisville, Kentucky, investors, headed by W. S. Peters, who signed a series of contracts with the Republic of Texas between 1841 and 1843. The Republic, anxious to encourage settlement in this region, granted over ten million acres of land to the company, including all of what was to become Dallas County except a ten-mile strip along the eastern edge. The Peters Colony, as this land was commonly called, extended north to the Red River and west nearly 200 miles. The company was responsible for surveying the properties and providing assistance in house construction. As an inducement to settle in the colony, each head of a family who met the conditions of settlement could claim homestead rights on 640 acres, and each single man or woman on 320 acres. The Peters Colony was widely advertised in both the United States and Europe, and eventually attracted nearly 3,000 settlers to Texas.

The company's broadsides make somewhat amusing reading today. According to the promoters, North Central Texas possessed a "mild and beautiful" climate, which "for health and pleasure, is not surpassed by any in the world, and in this respect may be termed the Italy of America." It might also interest modern residents of Dallas to read that—according to this broadside—the Trinity River was navigable all the way to Galveston Bay.[4]

Meanwhile, a frontiersman named John Neely Bryan had already selected the region as a likely spot for settlement. Like many men of his age and time, Bryan had led a rather nomadic existence. Born December 21, 1810, at Fayetteville, Tennessee, he studied law, was admitted to the bar, and moved to Memphis. In 1833 he contracted cholera and sought to recover his health in the Arkansas wilderness, living among the Cherokee Indians. Four years later he was in Van Buren, Arkansas, a trading center, where he bought and traded building lots. In 1839 he traveled southwest to Holland Coffee's trading post on the Red River where he clerked. Here he heard about the uninhabited land in the region called the Three Forks of the Trinity.

Exploring, he found a bluff overlooking a natural ford. Here the Trinity River, which could be an impassable barrier of mud

John Neely Bryan, the founder of Dallas, married Margaret Beeman, daughter of a pioneer family, in 1843. *Courtesy Dallas Historical Society.*

and water, narrowed like an hourglass over a formation of Austin chalk, providing a rock ford. This ford was already the intersection of two major Indian traces and would clearly be important for settlers moving into the region. There is a tradition that Bryan originally planned to establish a trading post here. With his experience as a land speculator in Van Buren, he may also have envisioned a town. In either case, he grasped the potential for profit in the site. Marking his claim with a stick and some stones, he returned to Fort Smith to close out some business, and in the fall of 1841 he set out for Texas again. Arriving at his bluff in late November, he built some sort of crude shelter and settled in.[5]

Several things had happened since his first visit which boded well for Bryan's plans. The government of the Republic had recently cleared most of the Indians from the region and had built Bird's Fort (close to modern Irving) to provide protection. William G. Cooke was employed to survey a highway along the Preston Trail, running from Coffee's Station on the Red River to a point just north of Bryan's site, and then a Central National Road northeast from there to Paris in Red River County. The Republic had also entered into the first of its contracts with the Peters Company to encourage settlement in the region. This, of course, was a mixed blessing for Bryan, since he was, in effect, squatting on Peters Colony land. It took several years for him to legitimize his claim.

Apparently it didn't take Bryan long to decide to found a town. In January 1842, he traveled up the West Fork of the Trinity to Bird's Fort and persuaded the Gilbert and Beeman families, who had been having problems with Indians, to leave and join him at his bluff. According to James J. Beeman, Bryan described the site and town he intended to build there and "was very anxious for us to move down."[6]

As it happened, the Beemans eventually settled along White Rock Creek, and the Gilberts moved elsewhere after two years. Bryan's problem was to convince people to take a lot in his "town" rather than file for their own 640-acre headright elsewhere in the Peters Colony. One story is that he offered a free lot to every newly married couple.[7] Another story is that he offered a lot as a prize in a contest to name the town, and that Charity Gilbert won it by suggesting "Dallas" in honor of Commodore Alexander Dallas, a well-known naval hero, who was supposed to have fired the first shot in the War of 1812. This name would, so the story goes, symbolize the town's intended destiny of commercial greatness through river transport.[8] The town may also have been named for George Mifflin Dallas, the Commodore's brother, who was elected vice president of the United States in 1844 with President James K. Polk, on a platform advocating annexation of Texas to the Union. Whatever its origins, the name Dallas appeared in deed records in August 1842,[9] in a diary written in the summer of 1843, and in a Houston newspaper in November 1843.[10]

While John Neely Bryan was trying to create a town, the other settlers moving into the area were busy clearing land for crops, building pens for animals, and erecting homes. Their major problem was transporting goods and people in and out of the area. The two roads laid out by the Republic, the Preston Road and the Central National Road, from Dallas to the Red River, were probably accurately described by one observer as "universally primitive."[11] Crossing the numerous streams could be treacherous. One early settler recalled, "There were no bridges or graded roads. When travelers came to one of those rushing streams they just had to wait until the water went down. Getting up and down those steep muddy banks was a hard problem. Wagons would often stick to the hubs. With each wheel loaded with sticky black mud that had to be pried off with poles, the teams had to be doubled and hitched to a wagon to get across."[12]

One of John Neely Bryan's first enterprises was a ferry operating across the Trinity River. John Beldon Billingsley, whose family spent several days in the village of Dallas in March 1844, was unimpressed. Billingsley described the ferry as "three cotton wood canoes placed parallel with each other and floored over with slabs." "It was pulled," he recalled, "by a buffalo wool rope tied to trees on each side of the river." His family had to unload their wagons to get across, and the cows and oxen had to swim.[13]

Lacking river or rail transportation, pioneers had to haul goods overland, usually from Jefferson, which was the closest river port. In February 1846, J. W. Smith and James M. Patterson decided to open a general store in Dallas. They bought their first load of supplies in Shreveport, and it took them forty days to make the 200-mile trip, swimming their oxen over the intervening streams and floating the two wagons and goods on rafts constructed for the purpose.[14]

Life on the sparsely populated frontier could be very lonely. Churches helped develop the ties of community. When Isaac Webb and his wife settled at Farmers Branch in 1844, they found a kindred Methodist spirit in Mrs. Nancy Jane Cochran. But all the other men in the area were, in Webb's words, "Sunday hunters." When they "would go a hunting," Webb recorded in his diary, "I would call the families together and read, sing and pray and instruct them the best I could. I was determined to stick to my beloved Methodism."[15] Webb wrote a friend of his near Clarksville asking for a preacher, and "sure enough in a few weeks Thomas Brown a preacher rode up to the settlement with his gun a liting before him inquiring for Webb." Brown stayed the night with the Webb family and preached what Webb believed to be the first sermon in the region.

That fall Webb was instrumental in organizing the first camp meeting in the county. Four families pitched tents, and four ministers gave sermons. "We had good preaching and quite a happy time and some accessions to the church," Webb wrote. Finally, in the spring of 1845, they put up an eighteen-foot-square church, made of hewed logs and covered with four-foot clapboards. Located 200 yards from Webb's house, this first church in the region was called Webb's Chapel in honor of the devout Methodist.

The other institution which helped bind a community and perpetuate its values was the school. According to one early history of Dallas County, the first formal school was taught in the Webb's Chapel building by Thomas C. Williams in February, March, and April of 1845.[16] Early schools, however, were extremely tenuous, dependent on the availability of a teacher and the ability of the parents to pay him, and operating only when the children weren't needed at home for planting or harvesting.

In 1845 a majority of Dallas voters—twenty-nine out of thirty-two—voted in favor of annexation with the United States. Like their brothers throughout Texas, they felt the time had come to sacrifice their independence as a Republic to the advantages of union with their powerful neighbor. During 1846 John Neely Bryan was kept busy setting up the government for the newly created Dallas County, and the political history of the region entered a new chapter.[17] It's perhaps significant that the first recorded celebration of Independence Day in Dallas took place on July 4, 1846.[18]

The entry of Texas into the Union encouraged immigration. By 1850, the population of Dallas County was 2,743 (163 in the town). Many were born in Georgia or Alabama and had immigrated to Tennessee and Missouri for a few years before coming down through Arkansas and across the Red River into North Texas. Nearly all the men were farmers by occupation, although some also had a specialty such as blacksmithing or milling. Foreign immigrants were also enticed to the area by the glowing reports of pioneers, speculators, and land companies. The 1850 Census listed two Germans, one a farmer and the other a blacksmith, and about a dozen people born in England or Ireland. The English included a shoemaker, a plasterer, and a millwright.

In 1853 a Frenchman named Victor Considerant arrived in Texas looking for a suitable place in which to found a socialist utopian community based on the ideals of Charles Fourier, who had died in 1837. The fertile lands of North Central Texas in springtime captivated Considerant. He returned to France, wrote a promotional book entitled *Au Texas*, and helped organize an emigration company. Early in 1855, 200 French and French-speaking Swiss and Belgians landed at Galveston after a stop in New Orleans. They made the overland portion of their journey from Galveston via Houston by wagon train, hiring as a guide a farmer living near Dallas who had come to Houston to sell two bales of cotton. The trip from Houston to Dallas took almost four weeks.[19]

In April the colonists arrived at Considerant's chosen spot in the limestone hills three miles west of Dallas. Here they organized themselves according to the Fourier system, calling their community La Reunion. Within three years the community had failed, through a combination of inadequate skills, bad weather, poor leadership, and internal dissension. But many of the colonists moved into Dallas, bringing with them diverse skills and a level of cultural refinement not usually found in frontier towns.[20]

Not all the early settlers came by choice. African Americans had entered the county as early as whites, but as slaves. The Mabel Gilbert family, whom John Neely Bryan persuaded to join him at his settlement in 1842, brought with them a young male slave identified only as "Smith."[21] The following year Allen (Al) Huitt accompanied his master John Huitt to Cedar Springs. A skilled blacksmith, Al Huitt became an important figure in Dallas County; as late as 1875 the City Directory mentioned, "Old Allen still lives in Dallas County, a venerable and respected citizen."[22]

According to the Federal Census, in 1850 there were 207 slaves in Dallas County. They were owned by 56 individuals—or 2 percent of the white population of 2,536. Most slave owners were engaged in agriculture, although slaves were also owned by two lawyers, two physicians, two wagon makers, two merchants, one inn keeper, and one tailor. The majority of slave owners possessed fewer than four slaves; only thirteen owned more than ten, and none owned more than twenty. There were no slave markets in Dallas, but slaves could be purchased privately or imported from elsewhere.[23]

Although the region remained overwhelmingly agricultural, business and even industry (on a small scale) were also developing. Dallas's first French immigrant, Maxime Guillot, opened the first factory, manufacturing carriages and wagons. Adolph Gouhenant, another immigrant, opened a picture gallery; the Caruth brothers (William and Walter) opened a general store; and Thomas Crutchfield opened a hotel. There were also an insurance agency, a boot and shoe shop, a milliner, two brickyards and two saddle shops.[24]

Dallas's business leaders, however, were Alexander and Sarah Cockrell. Alexander was a native of Kentucky who moved to Missouri and later to the Indian Territory, where he lived with the Cherokees. He joined his cousin in the Mountain Creek area west of the Trinity River in 1845, fought in the Mexican War, and received 640 acres of his own in southwest Dallas County. There he farmed and raised livestock and established a freighting business. Because he was illiterate, Alexander relied on his wife, Sarah Horton Cockrell, for writing, reading, and preparing business documents.

In 1852 Cockrell agreed to pay John Neely Bryan $7,000 for what remained of Bryan's property in Dallas. Alexander and Sarah left Mountain Creek and moved into Dallas. Alexander's first project was erecting a covered bridge across the Trinity River to replace Bryan's old ferry. This made transportation across the river far more convenient, and since it was a toll bridge, it was extremely lucrative for Cockrell.

Cockrell also built a steam sawmill at the foot of Commerce Street. The availability of sawn lumber created a demand for contractors, mechanics, carpenters, and masons, as well as investors. Cockrell started construction of a fancy new hotel, although he was killed before it was completed. In the spring of 1858 he was gunned down on the street by the town marshal, who owed him money.[25] However, his widow, Sarah, completed the hotel, which she named the St. Nicholas, and she continued to operate the other businesses.[26]

Alexander Cockrell's son once compared his father and John Neely Bryan. Bryan, he said, was a "planner"; his father was a "builder."[27] Bryan had the imagination to envision a town on the banks of the Trinity, but it took Cockrell to help bring it to fruition.[28]

Dallas was chartered as a town on February 2, 1856. Its boundaries embraced Bryan's original survey of one-half square mile. The first elections for municipal officers were held April 5, with fewer than 100 voters participating. Dr. Samuel Pryor, who supplemented his medical income by operating a drug store, was elected Mayor, receiving fifty-eight votes to thirty-four for Dr. A. A. Rice.[29] Dr. Pryor was described as "a portly man, weighing about 200 pounds, with a full beard and impressed you as a mover."[30]

The town of Dallas was already the county seat, having been chosen in 1850 by voters over Hord's Ridge (now Oak Cliff) and Cedar Springs. Its selection as county seat was critical to the growth of Dallas and to its gradual but steady development as the dominant town in the county. Anybody with legal business to conduct—whether it be a lawsuit or applying for a marriage license—had to come into town to the courthouse. Lawyers conducted most of their business at the courthouse and usually tried to office nearby. Citizens were summoned to the courthouse to serve on juries or as witnesses or defendants in lawsuits. All this activity was a boon to the hotels and boarding houses, general stores and saloons—all the businesses around the courthouse square. In 1855 the two-room log courthouse built in 1850 was replaced by a two-story brick building—probably the first in Dallas—fifty feet square. It was easily, and appropriately, the most impressive structure in town.

Part of the civilizing process of the frontier was the gradual imposition of law and order. In 1846 the state legislature created the Sixth Judicial District, composed of Dallas and five other

The selection of Dallas as county seat in 1850 was crucial to its early growth. The courthouse square is indicated by the scales of justice on this 1850 plat map. *Courtesy Dallas Historical Society.*

counties. Court was to be held in Dallas beginning on the first Monday in June and December and continue one week. The first grand jury in Dallas County brought sixty-one indictments, including fifty-one for gaming, one for murder, one for challenging to a duel, and four for assault and battery. The first civil suit was heard in December 1846, with Charlotte M. Dalton suing Joseph B. Dalton for divorce. The jury granted the divorce, and a few hours later Mrs. Dalton married Henderson Crouch, a member of the jury.

As the 1850s drew to a close, the citizens of Dallas could look with pride on the growth of their town from John Neely Bryan's single tent to a bustling county seat in less than twenty years. They still felt isolated, however. "While our granaries are teaming with the wealth of the finest soil in the Union," complained the Dallas *Herald*, the weekly newspaper which had been established in 1849, "they remain land-locked and their treasures literally rotting from the want of consumers and the proper mode of transportation."[31] In 1849 Bryan and two other men represented Dallas at a conference at Huntsville to discuss making the Trinity River navigable to the Gulf of Mexico, but the project came to nothing.[32] In 1852 a group of merchants hired Adam Haught to pilot an oar-powered flatboat, the *Dallas*, down the river carrying 134 bales of cotton. Hampered in its progress by countless snags and debris in the river, the *Dallas* got as far as Porter's Bluff, where shallow water downstream forced the crew to unload the cargo, and where the boat sank.[33]

Freight companies that had contracts with the U.S. government gave a boost to the local economy when they passed through Dallas and loaded their wagons with hundreds of pounds of flour. By the mid-1850s, travelers enjoyed stagecoach service from Dallas to Shreveport, and later to other destinations. Stage lines also carried mail, adding another important link to the outside world. Although freighters and stagecoaches improved the transportation of goods and people greatly, they remained slow, expensive, and inefficient. The ultimate solution to the region's transportation problems, as all the pioneers recognized, was the railroad. In 1848 the Houston & Texas Central (H&TC) acquired a charter to build a line north from Galveston Bay to the Red River, but work was agonizingly slow. The exact route was also uncertain, and Dallas could not be sure that it would be included. Before the railroad got much beyond Houston, however, Dallas and the rest of Texas and the nation were plunged into the Civil War.

In 1860 the population of Dallas County stood at 8,665. This was nearly a four-fold increase over the population of 2,743 ten years earlier. The population of the town of Dallas had increased even more dramatically, from 163 in 1850 to 775 in 1860. By far the majority of these folks were farmers. Dallas County was the leading wheat producer in the entire state of Texas, growing more than 194,000 bushels in 1860.

The type of agriculture practiced in Dallas County did not demand the intense, hard labor of cotton farming, and thus the demand for slave labor was far less than in the southeastern part of Texas. But the prevailing sentiment—at least as expressed in the weekly newspaper, the Dallas *Herald*—seems to have been stridently pro-slavery. There were periodic notices in the paper for runaway slaves, and whites who were caught trying to aid runaways were thrown into jail, and sometimes run out of the county altogether.[34]

The newspapers in Dallas and elsewhere in Texas fanned fears of a slave insurrection, fomented by outside agitators, the northern abolitionists. The fears seemed to be realized on the afternoon of July 8, 1860. It was a Sunday, and the temperature stood at 105 degrees. About 2 P.M. a sudden fire erupted in a box of wood shavings in front of W. W. Peak & Sons Drug Store on the east side of the courthouse square. In five minutes the entire building was on fire. Except for the two-story brick courthouse in the middle of the square, nearly all the buildings in Dallas at the time were built of wood, and in the dry, 105-degree heat of a July afternoon, the other buildings lining the square quickly went up in flames. Every store, both hotels, the Dallas *Herald* office, the post office—twenty-five establishments in all—were destroyed in a couple of hours. Private residences beyond the square were saved, but the destruction was a profound shock to a town that had come so far in less than twenty years.

Then it was learned that the same afternoon as the Dallas fire, fires had erupted in Denton, Pilot Point, Honey Grove, Jefferson, Austin, and other Texas towns. This looked suspiciously like a conspiracy, perhaps the onset of the feared insurrection. In Dallas County and elsewhere throughout North and Central Texas, vigilance committees were formed to identify the plotters. Charles Pryor, editor of the Dallas *Herald*, wrote an article claiming that abolitionist preachers had devised a "deep laid scheme of villainy" to devastate all of North Texas by fire and assassination, then to enlist the Indians to launch a war to free the slaves.[35]

This two-story brick courthouse was constructed in 1857 and torn down in 1871. It was the only building at the square to escape destruction in the fire of 1860. *Courtesy Dallas Public Library.*

The vigilance committee for Dallas County interrogated nearly a hundred slaves and identified three as ringleaders in a plot. On July 23, two weeks after the fire, a committee of fifty-two leading citizens met behind closed doors to assess punishment. They sentenced the three slaves (Cato, Patrick, and Sam Smith) to be hung and every other slave in the county to be whipped. The three men were hanged the next afternoon on the banks of the Trinity River. Two Iowa preachers, believed to have been the agents in charge of the insurrection plot in Dallas County, were jailed, publicly whipped, and ordered out of the county.[36]

Rebuilding started immediately. By the end of the year the newspaper declared, "Within six months Dallas has risen almost like a dream from its ruins."[37] The election of Abraham Lincoln as president in November 1860, however, added momentum to the call that had been building for some time for the Southern states to secede from the Union. At a mass meeting at the courthouse, a resolution was unanimously adopted which declared that "the people of Dallas County will not submit to an administration of the government by Abraham Lincoln."[38] The Dallas Light Artillery, a volunteer company, was raised, along with local militia. Dallas sent four delegates to a secession convention in Austin in late January 1861, where they voted with the majority to withdraw from the Union. When voters went to the polls on February 23, Dallas men voted 741 to 237 to secede.

Once the war began, enthusiasm for the cause ran high. Enlistment in cavalry and artillery companies was brisk, with nearly one out of three eligible Dallas County men serving in the Confederate forces at some time. The county voted 516 to 3 to contribute to the Confederacy $5,000 in gold held in the county treasury. Later the Confederate government designated Dallas as a general quartermaster and commissary headquarters for the collection of food and supplies.

Dallas was never the scene of actual warfare, but its residents were affected by the shortage of many products. "There is little market for anything," Susan Good wrote her husband, Capt. John Good, on September 22, 1861. "Money is scarcer than ever known. Many would be glad to sell wheat at 50 cts a bush[el] if they could get the money in hand. All the farmers can do is to exchange their produce at reduced prices to the merchants and pay 100 percent more on the goods than they have been in the habit of paying."[39]

It could be argued that the Civil War was the first national event that had a direct impact on Dallas. The second was the Reconstruction period that followed. In Dallas, opposition to Reconstruction policies focused on the Freedmen's Bureau, the agency set up by Congress in 1865 to assist African Americans in their adjustment to freedom.

The first Freedmen's Bureau agent assigned to Dallas, Lt. William H. Horton, did not assume his duties until May of 1867. From the beginning he faced a hostile climate. He drafted and tried to enforce a written labor contract that outlined terms of employment and wages for freedmen, many of whom were still working for their former masters without pay, or on shares for part of a crop. But the local courts refused to enforce such contracts, and Horton eventually had to rely on arresting violators and fining them in his own office.[40]

Horton faced his greatest opposition when trying to prosecute whites for acts of violence against African Americans. The courts refused to convict whites despite strong evidence. Horton increasingly took the law into his own hands, establishing a sort of administrative court of his own. His opponents fought back, bringing suit against him in District Court for false imprisonment. Bowing to pressure, the military authorities transferred Horton to Bastrop and then gave him a dishonorable discharge. Horton's successor as Freedmen's Bureau agent was murdered, and the next one stayed in Lancaster, in southern Dallas County, and rarely ventured into Dallas.

Dallas was in fact undergoing a vast transformation. A Dallas resident who left before the Civil War, or even immediately after it, and didn't return until the early 1870s would hardly have recognized the place. Dallas had become a boom town. Promotion of the area rivaled that of the Peters Colony twenty-five years earlier. "The business it [Dallas] does in dry goods, groceries, blacksmithing, foundrying, wagons, buggy, plow, cultivator and saddlery making, milling, wool-carding, cotton-ginning, brickmaking, concreting, etc., etc., is so large and remunerative," wrote the newspaper editor in 1870, "that but a single glance at the advertisements . . . found in the Dallas *Herald*—must satisfy the most incredulous and distant reader that our flattering statements of the importance of Dallas are anything but fiction."[41] There was a spirit of optimism and excitement in the town. "Dallas is improving very rapidly," a young attorney wrote his brother in 1871. "The prospects now are very flattering indeed. . . . Emigration [*sic*] pouring in and everybody talking about the town."[42]

The reason was simple but fundamental: the railroads were finally on their way to Dallas.

2.
A BOOM TOWN

CONSTRUCTION OF THE Houston & Texas Central railroad resumed after the Civil War, and within a few years Dallas began experiencing some of the differences rail transport could make. Instead of goods being shipped from New Orleans up the Red River to Jefferson and then overland, they now tended to come through Houston and up the railroad to whatever the northernmost terminal happened to be, then loaded on wagons for delivery to North Texas.

The exact route which the railroad planned to take was not precisely fixed. But Dallas citizens were determined that it would be through their town. As early as 1866, there was a community meeting, presided over by John Neely Bryan himself, to discuss strategies for attracting a railroad. In 1871, when it appeared that the H&TC might lay its tracks eight miles east of Dallas, town leaders met with railroad officials to see what it would take to persuade them to route closer to town. The railroad owners asked for free right-of-way for their tracks and enough property for a depot, and they expected a cash grant. Dallas voters were asked to approve these inducements, and by an overwhelming vote of 177 to 11, they did so. The H&TC got 115 acres of land, including the right-of-way that is today Central Expressway, and $5,000 in cash.[43]

Meanwhile, Dallas citizens had also become excited at the prospect of enticing the Texas & Pacific railroad, which was building the southern transcontinental route to the Pacific Ocean across Texas, to cross the H&TC at Dallas. Having one railroad would insure the continued economic growth of the town, but to become the first rail crossroads in Texas, the site where an east-west line crossed a north-south one, practically guaranteed economic dominance of the region.

Unfortunately, T&P officials seemed more interested in routing the railroad across the 32nd parallel, which is fifty miles south of Dallas, closer to modern-day Corsicana. Dallas leaders were not about to let this golden opportunity pass them by. The Texas legislature was engaged in formulating a bill which would grant rights-of-way to the T&P across the state. A typical part of such a bill was provision for the railroad to pass near various water sources, such as springs, so that it could be easily supplied. Dallas leaders instructed John V. Lane, their representative in the legislature, to add a rider to the bill requiring the T&P to pass within one mile of Browder's Springs.[44] In the rush to pass the bill, nobody bothered to find out exactly where Browder's Springs was located. Only after the bill was passed and the legislature adjourned, was it realized that Browder's Springs was one mile south of the Dallas County Courthouse, in what is today Old City Park.

T&P officials were furious, and they threatened to lay the tracks one mile *south* of Browder's Springs, rather than north of the springs as Dallas had wanted. This would have put the tracks an inconvenient two miles south of the business district. Dallas leaders quickly consulted with the railroad officials to see what they could do to soothe their feelings. Like the Houston & Texas Central owners, the T&P crowd wanted free right of way through town and land for a depot. But their cash demand was considerably higher—$5,000 in cash *plus* $100,000 in bonds. Nevertheless, Dallas voters approved this proposition by a vote of 192 to 0. The town even changed the name of Burleson Avenue, where the T&P planned to lay its tracks, to Pacific Avenue.[45]

July 16, 1872, was one of those red-letter days in Dallas history. On that day, a Houston & Texas Central locomotive, drawing a string of lumber-laden flat cars and a single passenger car at the rear, chugged into Dallas. It was greeted by a cheering throng of

Widowed at the age of thirty-eight, Sarah Horton Cockrell took over her husband's business interests and became Dallas's leading entrepreneur. Photograph circa 1890. *Courtesy Dallas Historical Society.*

4,000–5,000 people, followed by an afternoon of speechmaking and celebrating. John Neely Bryan, in what may have been his last public appearance, was on the platform with other dignitaries.[46] "We feel hundreds of miles nearer home and no longer behind the times," one man wrote his parents in Illinois. "Dallas is to be grinned at no longer as a one horse town. It has put away its petticoats and donned a new pair of 'britches' with pockets and a cigar in its mouth and is no longer a little boy. . . ."[47]

Dallas gained two other significant links with the world in 1872. A week before the Houston & Texas Central reached Dallas, the telegraph lines, which tended to accompany the railroad, were brought into town. On July 8, Mayor Henry Ervay wired the mayors of Galveston, Houston, Austin, San Antonio, and Brownsville: "We are this day placed in telegraphic communication with the whole national public, thanks to the arrival of the Iron Horse."[48]

A third link between Dallas and the outer world was also completed in 1872, an iron bridge across the Trinity River at the foot of Commerce Street. Erected at a cost of $65,000 by a company headed by Sarah Horton Cockrell, and with ironwork manufactured in St. Louis, the new bridge measured 300 feet in length. The fact that it was a toll bridge (five cents for pedestrians) angered farmers to the west. Ten years later the city purchased the bridge for $41,600 and opened it to the public free of charge.[49] But whether toll or free, the bridge greatly facilitated the ability of farmers and others living west of the Trinity to get their produce into the city, and, thus, to the railroad depot for shipment.

The fact that the Houston & Texas Central depot was a mile east of the courthouse—about where Main Street crosses Central Expressway today—encouraged the development of a street railway system to link the old business center with the depot and all the activity building up around it. Local businessmen subscribed $10,000 to capitalize the Dallas City Railroad Company, with a line running down Main Street. The line inaugurated service on February 7, 1873, with two cars, each ten feet long, pulled by two mules. Early service could be erratic, especially when the mules got frightened and ran away.[50]

The arrival of the railroads fulfilled the hopes of business and civic leaders—probably beyond their imaginations. Dallas became a boom town. The population soared, and land values skyrocketed, especially for property near the rail lines. The face of the town began to change almost overnight. More than 700 structures went up in one year.[51] Many of these were flimsy frame buildings, but the first city directory, published in November 1873, reported that during the first ten months of the year, over fifty large two- and three-story buildings had gone up, "some with iron fronts, some with stone."[52]

Like Atlanta, Dallas found itself in a strategic geographical location for the trade and transportation of its abundant regional products to northern and eastern manufacturing plants. The blackland soil had always been attractive to cotton growers, but without rail or river transport, there had been no economical way to ship bales of cotton out of the area. Now cotton became the region's principal cash crop, and Elm Street in Dallas was its market.

Dallas also became headquarters for a number of merchants, operators of what we would today call department stores. These men are usually called "terminus merchants," because they had followed the Houston & Texas Central railroad as it built north from the Gulf, opening stores at each terminal town along the way. When the railroad finally reached Dallas, they recognized that Dallas would be the dominant city for all of North Texas, and so they opened their flagship stores here. They were mostly German Jewish merchants, some of whom had worked in New York and the East before coming to Texas. They included Alexander and Philip Sanger, who opened Sanger Brothers Store, and Emanuel Kahn, who also opened a general store.[53] Area residents could now obtain organs and pianos, books and stationery, jewelry and watches at remarkably low prices.[54] New jobs were created for store clerks, bank tellers, and teamsters, as the economy began to diversify.

As with most frontier boom towns, Dallas was inundated with single men, eager to prosper economically, but many also patrons of gambling halls, saloons, and brothels. The 1870s were years of

E. M. Kahn (far left) and Sanger Brothers were among the terminus merchants who opened stores in Dallas after the arrival of the railroad in 1872. Their stores were at the corner of Main and Lamar Streets. *Courtesy Dallas Historical Society.*

gunfighters and train robbers, pickpockets and burglars, drunks and con men.[55] The first city directory listed more saloons than any other business.[56]

The Board of Aldermen wrestled not only with the crime problem, but also with the difficulties associated with providing services to the rapidly growing population. Within a decade, Dallas had taken over the privately owned waterworks and the volunteer fire department. Citizens also enjoyed a new public park—City Park—and telephone service.

The railroads had made it easier not only to transport goods in and out of Dallas but also to transport people, and as a result the 1870s and 1880s became a period of great migration into the city not only of people from other parts of the United States seeking jobs and opportunity, but also of foreign immigrants. The German colony spawned a number of businesses and establishments catering to their special interests, such as Simon Mayer's beer garden, which included a small zoo; breweries and ice houses; bakeries; and German-language newspapers and magazines.[57] Swiss immigrants established some of the first dairies in Dallas.[58]

Italians came in the 1880s to work on the railroads and stayed to open businesses, becoming especially prominent in groceries and food-related industries. Nicolo Nigra received one of the first shipments of refrigerated bananas. The DeStefanos developed a large wholesale fruit and produce market. The Italian community developed its own Italian-language press as well as benevolent and fraternal organizations.[59]

Mexican sheepherders were reported passing through Dallas in 1859. Other Hispanics operated ox-carts which transported goods between Dallas and San Antonio. The first influx of Hispanic settlers was in the 1870s, with railroad section crewmen. The 1875 Dallas city directory lists Hispanic merchants, clerks, and physicians. By the turn of the century, Mexican Americans were working as grocers, vendors, cotton buyers, printers, candy manufacturers, and tailors. Tamale vendors were seen on the streets in the 1880s, and the first Mexican restaurant opened then.[60]

Despite racial segregation and the political disfranchisement that African Americans confronted in Dallas, their community grew and thrived. The city's black population grew from 1,921 in 1880 to 8,061 in 1890. Their percentage in the total population during this period grew from 18.5 percent to 21.17 percent. African American family life benefited from the establishment of churches and neighborhoods. African American children were provided with public schools when free schools were instituted in 1878, but they were segregated because separate schools for "colored" had been mandated by the state's School Laws of 1876 and 1884. Black students had poorer facilities and fewer teachers per pupil than white children. There were no libraries in black schools, because the school board considered the buildings "insecure," and African American children were given only sixty days of instruction each year, compared to 100 for whites.[61]

As for public education in general, Dallas voters consistently

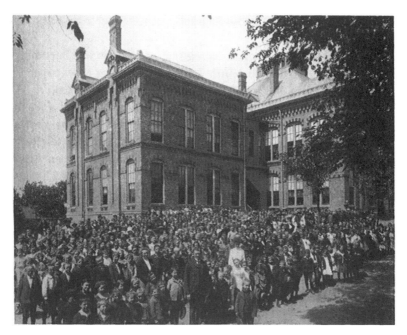

Dallas public schools were overcrowded from the day they opened in 1884. The Oak Grove School was built in 1889 at the southeast corner of S. Harwood and Jackson Streets and was torn down in 1915. *Courtesy Dallas Historical Society.*

defeated proposals for school taxes, which meant that schools met in rented buildings, with no money for books, desks, or bookcases. Not until 1884, when the state legislature amended the law to allow school districts to levy taxes, was a Dallas Board of School Trustees (later called the Board of Education) organized. With authority from the city council, the board hired a superintendent. When the school term began in September, there were ten grades, and students were packed into six two-story white frame schoolhouses, heated by wood or coal stoves and with no indoor plumbing. So many students enrolled that the first three grades had to attend in split shifts; the next year the fifth, sixth, and seventh grades moved into a rented room over a grocery store on Elm Street. Conditions there were not conducive to learning, as the principal reported that "noises from the street were distressing" and "it was frequently impossible for one, speaking in an ordinary tone, to be heard at all."[62]

Nevertheless, literacy was increasing, and Dallas was becoming the publishing center for North Texas. The leading newspaper in Texas in the early 1880s was the Galveston *Daily News*. Col. A. H. Belo, the owner, decided that North Texas was a ripe area in which to establish a sister paper. In the early 1880s he sent a young manager, George Bannerman Dealey, to scout the territory and determine the best site in which to locate a new paper. After surveying all the towns in the region, Dealey recommended Dallas and predicted a beginning circulation of 5,000, rising to 15,000 in a few years. In the summer of 1885, Dealey was sent to Dallas to head the operation. No expense was spared to make the Dallas *Morning News*, as the new paper was to be called, a first-class operation. An eight-page, web-perfecting Bullock press was installed which could print 100 copies a minute. The new office awed Dallasites with its display of 100 Edison incandescent light bulbs. The first issue appeared, on schedule, on October 1, 1885.[63] Three years later readers gained a new afternoon paper, the Dallas *Daily Times Herald*, the product of a merger between the old Dallas *Daily Times* (1879) and the Dallas *Daily* (Evening) *Herald*, a paper started in January 1886. The *News* and the *Times Herald* were to be (mostly) friendly rivals for more than a century.[64]

In 1886 a group of Dallas businessmen, under the leadership of banker William Henry Gaston, received a charter to hold the Dallas State Fair and Exposition. Agricultural and mechanical fairs had been held in Dallas as early as 1859, providing opportunities for farmers and ranchers to buy and sell livestock and to inspect the newest implements. But the early fairs were sporadic. There was no organization to stage a large, multi-faceted fair on an annual basis. This was what Gaston and his associates provided in 1886.

From the beginning the State Fair attracted large numbers of people from throughout Texas each October to view livestock exhibits, enjoy band concerts and recitals, defy gravity on amusement rides, and gape at the latest technological gadgets. The governor of Texas usually opened the fair, and such national figures

The State Fair drew thousands of visitors to Dallas each October beginning in 1886. Horse racing was the primary attraction in the early years. *Courtesy Dallas Historical Society.*

as Booker T. Washington (1900), Carrie Nation (1902), U.S. Vice President Charles W. Fairbanks (1907), President William Howard Taft (1909), and New Jersey Governor Woodrow Wilson (1911) delivered addresses at the fair during its first quarter century. Visitors were exposed to everything from Grand Baby Contests to suffrage lectures, and hot air balloons to automobile races.[65]

The hundreds of thousands of annual visitors were a boon to Dallas barbers, livery men, saloon keepers, hack and express drivers, restaurants, hotels, and boarding houses. Many visitors chose to settle permanently in Dallas. The cultural life of the city received an annual boost by the presence of such performers as opera singer Marcella Sembrich and band leader John Philip Sousa. The region's farmers benefited from exposure to new agricultural technology, and livestock breeds gradually improved through the livestock competitions.[66] After the city purchased the fairgrounds in 1904, they became a year-round park, with some permanent amusement rides, a skating rink, and an art gallery.

By 1890 Dallas boasted most of the trappings of a major urban center: public utilities, public schools, daily newspapers, the State Fair. It was also, for the first and only time, the largest city in Texas as measured by the Federal Census, with a population of 38,067. But by 1900 it had dropped to third place, behind San Antonio and Houston, as it wrestled with the social and economic problems of a city that had grown too fast.

3.
GROWING PAINS

DALLASITES GREETED the new decade optimistically. Construction began for a new courthouse (the county's sixth), and for a new luxury hotel, the Oriental. In May 1893 citizens crowded the banks of the Trinity River to greet the steamboat *H. A. Harvey, Jr.*, which had traveled from Galveston in a mere two months.[67] But the United States was soon swept by a financial "panic," a recession triggered by the failure of the Philadelphia & Reading Railroad and a subsequent run on the banks. Five Dallas banks failed, and the price of cotton dropped to less than five cents a pound. Dallas's population actually declined.[68]

Dallas was one of the two most industrialized cities in Texas, and the recession hit it hard. A majority of laborers worked in three areas: the manufacture of leather goods (mostly harness and other farm equipment), printing and publishing, and machine-tool production. Poor working conditions in some of these industries had encouraged the organization of labor unions and occasional strikes.[69] The recession threw hundreds of men out of work and dealt a setback to the infant unionizing effort.

The city's aldermen struggled with problems such as crime, health care, and city services, but Dallas's rapid growth left many issues unresolved. Assuming the lead in attacking urban ills in Dallas were middle- and upper-class women, acting initially through literary clubs. Formed in the late 1880s, these clubs were

The Dallas Free Kindergartens, sponsored by several women's organizations, helped prepare children of working mothers for first grade. *Courtesy Dallas Public Library.*

part of a national trend, exposing women with leisure time not only to culture but also to social concerns.[70]

Because most of the clubwomen were wives and mothers, it is not surprising that they turned their attention toward issues affecting children. Of growing concern were the young children of women who worked in factories, or as seamstresses or domestic servants. Not only was there a problem of finding appropriate day care for these children, but when they entered school at age six, they were often found to be far behind other children in developmental skills. In 1901 the Dallas Free Kindergarten Association, an amalgamation of several free nurseries which had been established in working-class neighborhoods during the past two years, joined the Dallas Federation of Women's Clubs and began enjoying its support.

Specially trained teachers led the children in games, singing, nature study, arts and crafts, read stories aloud and taught basic housekeeping skills. The games and songs were actually practical exercises to prepare the children to enter public schools with the same skills as children who had attended private kindergartens.[71] In addition to caring for the children of working mothers, the kindergartens had as their goal providing general social services for the families of their charges. Soon the kindergartens were offering cooking and sewing lessons for children and their mothers, Boys Clubs to replace street gangs, and sites for neighborhood musical entertainments. One Neighborhood House, as it was called, was also the home of a Kindergarten Training School, where young women were trained as teachers and social settlement workers.[72]

The Dallas Federation of Women's Clubs also raised $10,000 to provide a public park with playground equipment, and paid the salaries of the first director and physical instructor until the city finally assumed responsibility. After investigating conditions in the local jails—where juveniles were routinely incarcerated with hardened criminals—the Federation worked with the county commissioners to persuade the state legislature to establish a system of juvenile courts in Texas. By 1910 the Federation had succeeded in persuading the city to hire a police matron and a probation officer, for both of whom the Federation initially paid the salaries.[73]

In 1908 two Dallas clubwomen, Mrs. E. P. Turner and Mrs. P. P. Tucker, ran for the school board and were elected. They were the first two women elected to public office in Dallas, and at a time when women themselves could not vote. Both women participated actively in all facets of running the school district, focusing their attention especially on better nutrition, sanitation, and cleanliness in the schools.[74]

From issues benefiting children, Dallas women soon tackled problems affecting public health. For some years there had been concern that local dairies were watering their milk. In order to have more to sell, farmers and dairymen often diluted milk with water, then added chalk to restore its appearance. President Theodore Roosevelt's signing of the Meat Inspection and Pure Food and Drug Act in 1906 inspired members of the Dallas Woman's Forum to lobby members of the Dallas City Council for a local act, which would include the appointment of an official chemist for the city to inspect dairy and other products. Despite opposition from dairy owners, farmers, grocers, and druggists, in December 1906 the Dallas City Council passed a comprehensive pure food and drug ordinance. The new law included provisions for the city chemist to inspect all places where food and drink were sold, prohibited the sale of "unwholesome, adulterated" products, and prescribed penalties for offenders.[75]

Women joined male civic leaders in forming the Cleaner Dallas League in 1899, advocating street cleaning, garbage collection, and more sanitary sewer connections.[76] Although the clean-up movement was inspired partly by a national interest in city beautification, at base it reflected a realization that the hitherto unplanned and unregulated growth of the city was endangering public health.[77]

Clubwomen also took the lead in establishing the city's major cultural institutions. In 1898 Mrs. Henry Exall, president of the Shakespeare Club, called together representatives of five women's clubs in Dallas to form the Dallas Federation of Women's Clubs, with an initial goal of obtaining a public library. A large public meeting was held on March 1, 1899, and a second a month later. Within six weeks, $12,000 had been raised from 1,000 contributors. Mrs. Exall and her brother, an attorney, then composed a letter to Andrew Carnegie, who had begun supporting the erection of libraries throughout the United States. He replied in September, agreeing to give $50,000 toward construction of a library building, if the city would donate a suitable site and pledge $4,000 annually toward operational support. The construction committee monitored the work so closely that the final costs came to $50,097, only $97 over the amount Carnegie had pledged. The new library opened with much fanfare on October 30, 1901, barely two and a half years after the Library Association had been formed. The new facility boasted 10,000 books on the shelves and modern, well-lit reading rooms.[78]

The construction of the new library provided the opportunity for fulfillment of another cultural dream, a permanent public art gallery. When the library was being planned, Frank Reaugh, a local artist, suggested that space be set aside for an art gallery, and the Library Association agreed. The day after the official opening of the library, an art show opened in the upstairs gallery, featuring mostly works that had recently been exhibited at the State Fair, but also including some paintings and sculpture by rising local artists. After another successful show a year later, Mrs. Exall and the library's board decided the time was ripe to organize an independent art association. This group began forming a permanent collection of art and mounting regular exhibitions, and within a few years had its own building at Fair Park, the forerunner of today's Dallas Museum of Art.[79]

The early growth of Dallas, like other cities, was limited geographically by the distance people could walk to and from work. Only the well-to-do could afford to keep a horse and buggy. Most businesses clustered around the courthouse square. A store owner and his family might live over the store, or behind it. There was no such thing as planned development, or zoning, and as a result, small and large houses might be mixed in with business establishments on the same block.[80]

What changed the spatial configuration of Dallas and other growing cities was the development of mass-transit systems. Gradually the streetcar lines began to be electrified and expanded, generally in cooperation with a land speculator or developer. As early as 1874, Edward Browder began promoting a new residential neighborhood on land he owned just south of town, between today's Farmers' Market and City Hall. In 1876 J. J. Eakins gave some land near Browder's Springs for a public park—called City Park—and a street railway line was planned running down Ervay Street to the park. More residential developments were created along the line, and soon this south-side area was known as The Cedars and boasted the finest homes in town—occupied by the Sanger brothers and other prominent people. The street railway offered them an easy, efficient means to get from home to work, and enabled them to insulate themselves somewhat from the noises and smells of downtown living.[81] When Thomas Marsalis began developing Oak Cliff on the west bank of the Trinity, he promoted it as the "Brooklyn of Dallas," and when Hugh Prather and Edgar Flippen planned their upscale Highland Park residential neighborhood north of town in 1907, they advertised it as "ten degrees cooler" than the city and removed from its "smoke and dust."[82]

Because fares to ride the street railways were generally kept low, the new mass-transit was also popular with the growing middle class—the clerks, bank tellers, stenographers, telephone operators, etc.—who were finding new jobs in the growing city. By the early 1900s, they, too, could find pleasant housing in planned residential subdivisions along a streetcar line, such as Munger Place and Junius Heights.[83] The introduction of the automobile after 1900 further facilitated the process.

The development of the so-called "streetcar suburbs" meant a fairly large expansion of the geographic boundaries of cities, and Dallas was no exception. Occupying less than one square mile in 1870, Dallas grew to nine square miles in 1890, and to twenty-three square miles by 1920.[84] Part of the dramatic growth in 1890 was due to the annexation of the formerly independent town of East Dallas. This annexation of small, nearby communities by a rapidly growing city was also common in the late nineteenth and early twentieth centuries. In 1903 Dallas annexed the town of Oak Cliff across the Trinity River.

By the turn of the century, the local economy had recovered, and Dallas was the leading book, drug, jewelry, and wholesale liquor market in the Southwest.[85] Its population stood at 42,638, but promoters were ambitious for more: in 1905 businessmen formed the 150,000 Club, aimed at boosting the city's population to 150,000 by 1910. Their slogan was "Dallas: The City of Splendid Realities." In 1907 Dallas gained its first steel skyscraper, the fifteen-story Praetorian Building, and Herbert Marcus, his sister Carrie Neiman, and her husband, Al, opened a women's specialty store called Neiman-Marcus.

That same year voters approved a change in the city's charter to institute a mayor-commission form of government, similar to that set up in Galveston to deal with the hurricane disaster of 1900 and subsequently copied by other Texas cities. With four commissioners heading such municipal departments as waterworks, police and fire, and public works, the new system was designed to streamline urban administration.[86]

The new commission was quickly put to the test when Dallas suffered one of its worst natural disasters. In May 1908 the Trinity

Dallas Consolidated Electric Street Railway Company

PIERRE S. duPONT, President
EDWARD T. MOORE, Secretary and Manager

Why bother with a horse and buggy, when by our Transfer System we will carry you to all the principal parts of the city for one fare

CAUTION ! Never get ON or OFF CAR until it is Stopped, and then always get on or off on the RIGHT HAND SIDE. Look Out for Approaching Cars. NEVER CROSS A TRACK until you are sure there is no danger

General Office and Transfer Station MAIN and MARKET STS.

OFFICE PHONE 255
CAR SHEDS PHONE 242

REACHES ALL THE PRINCIPAL POINTS IN THE CITY

The development of the streetcar system encouraged the geographic growth of Dallas and the construction of residential suburbs. *Courtesy Dallas Historical Society.*

A flood in 1908 destroyed all the bridges between Dallas and Oak Cliff and left 4,000 people homeless, but it did inspire civic leaders to commission the first city plan. *Courtesy Dallas Historical Society.*

River flooded, damaging much of the business district. The entire city was without electricity, water, and fire protection for several days; 4,000 people were made homeless; and all the bridges between Dallas and Oak Cliff were washed away.[87]

The devastation wreaked by the flood inspired G. B. Dealey, publisher of the Dallas *Morning News*, and other civic leaders to begin lobbying for a city plan for Dallas, much like those that had begun directing the growth of cities like Kansas City and St. Louis. In addition to a periodically dangerous river running through its midst, Dallas was plagued by congested downtown streets, often jogging at weird angles and blocked by railroad tracks. Nine railroads used five passenger stations scattered around downtown, there was no boulevard system, and far too little park space.[88]

The Dallas City Plan and Improvement League, a committee of the Chamber of Commerce, persuaded the city to hire George

Kessler, a noted landscape architect who had once lived in Dallas and helped design Fair Park. Kessler had more recently developed a city plan for Kansas City. His recommendations, published in 1912, called for straightening the Trinity and confining it within a levee system, building a Union Station to serve all the railroads, and removing the railroad tracks from Pacific Avenue. Voters had already approved bonds to construct the Houston Street viaduct, connecting the east and west banks of the Trinity. When it opened in 1912, Dallasites boasted that it was the longest concrete structure in the world. Union Station opened in 1916, and the Pacific tracks came up in 1921.[89] However, work didn't begin on the Trinity River levee project until 1929, and most of the boulevard and park system Kessler recommended was never completed.[90] Nevertheless, for the first time, Dallas was beginning to plan its growth in an orderly fashion.[91]

The decade of the 1910s saw progress on several fronts. White Rock Lake was constructed as the city's water reservoir, and a water-filtration plant was built. In 1914 Dallas was selected as the site for the Eleventh District of the Federal Reserve Bank, the smallest city in the nation to be so honored.[92] The city's banking capital doubled overnight, and its financial dominance extended throughout Texas and into surrounding states. Dallas's selection was the direct result of serious lobbying by civic leaders, as was the decision of the Methodist Episcopal Church, South, to locate a university in Dallas. This seat of higher learning, Southern Methodist University, opened in September 1915 with the largest opening enrollment (706) of any university up to that time except the University of Chicago.[93] The local economy thrived during World War I. Dallas was the world's largest inland cotton market, and the center of cotton-gin manufacturing. Citizens raised $7 million for the Liberty Loan Drive. The population soared— from 92,000 in 1910 to nearly 159,000 in 1920, raising Dallas from the fifty-eighth largest city in America to the forty-second.

But some profound changes were also taking place. In 1917 refugees from the Mexican Civil War immigrated to Dallas to form the city's first sizable Hispanic community. Dallas's African American population also grew, and was becoming more outspoken as "Jim Crow" laws became more pronounced. Dallas voters approved prohibition and women's suffrage amendments to the state constitution, and by 1920 Dallas ranked first among Texas cities in the percentage of women in the work force.

Such changes could not occur without some social disruption. Indeed, the 1920s were to be one of the most turbulent decades in Dallas's history.

4.
FROM TRAUMA
TO TRIUMPH

PROHIBITION PUT OUT OF business some 220 saloons and beer parlors in Dallas, as well as twelve wholesale liquor houses and a brewery. As elsewhere throughout the nation, private stills and bootleggers quickly began operations, often quite profitably; a 1925 survey revealed that Dallas bootleggers enjoyed a daily income of $36,000.[94] Throughout the 1920s the Dallas sheriff and his deputies were kept busy arresting violators and confiscating their wares.

Even more disturbing was the resurgence of the Ku Klux Klan. The Dallas chapter, organized in 1920, swelled within four years to become the largest in the nation, with an estimated 13,000 members. Although the Klan appealed to the uneducated, arousing hatred not only of African Americans but also of Catholics, Jews, and foreigners in general, many members in Dallas were leaders in banking, utilities, and other professions. At one time, the Dallas police commissioner and the chief of police were both members, as were the Democratic Party county chairman and the county tax collector. A local cut-rate dentist named Hiram Wesley Evans soon rose to take charge of the national Klan. In 1923 there was a special KKK day at the State Fair, where 25,000 spectators watched 5,631 men sworn into the Klan.[95]

For several years the Klan conducted a reign of terror in Dallas, kidnapping blacks whom they suspected of some behavior such as

Dallas Klan No. 66 Drum and Bugle Corps, a seventy-five-piece group, posed inside a square made up of Klansmen on "KKK Day" at the Texas State Fair in 1923. Dallas had the largest chapter of the Ku Klux Klan in the nation during the early 1920s. *Courtesy Dallas Public Library.*

consorting with white women, whipping them or tar-and-feathering them, and sometimes etching the initials KKK into their foreheads with acid. Prosecuting the perpetrators of such outrages in the justice system was hopeless, since the police and juries were packed with Klan members.

There were certainly many Dallas citizens who opposed the Klan and bravely spoke out against it. Leading the opposition was the Dallas *Morning News.* The Klan organized advertising boycotts against the *News,* accusing it of being controlled by Catholics (a primary Klan target). Agents for the paper were subject to threats of violence, and the paper suffered financially for its steady opposition to the Klan.[96]

In 1924 the Klan attempted unsuccessfully to win the governorship of Texas. But national publicity of the Klan's abuses had begun to turn public opinion against the organization, and within a fairly quick period, the Klan collapsed. Membership in Texas fell from nearly 100,000 to less than 20,000 by 1926.[97] Anti-Klan men regained control of city government, and the Dallas *Morning News* survived to become one of the leading newspapers in the state.

The collapse of the Klan by no means alleviated the prejudice faced by African Americans in Dallas. Employment opportunities were severely limited. The poll tax restricted their power at the ballot box. Streets in Dallas's black neighborhoods were unpaved, and the two parks designated for African Americans had no playground equipment. Public swimming pools were strictly forbidden to any but whites. There was only one high school for black students—Booker T. Washington High School, which opened in 1922. Designed to accommodate 800 students, it quickly had to house 1,600, and students were forced to attend on double shifts.

Despite Supreme Court rulings, Dallas housing remained rigidly segregated. As the African American population continued to grow, housing came to be in short supply, and much of it was abysmal. A survey conducted in 1924–1925 declared that a quarter of the city's African Americans were living in rental housing "unfit for human habitation." Sixty-six percent lacked a bath, toilet, or running water. Half the houses had no electricity or gas.[98]

Nevertheless, the African American community in Dallas developed one of the liveliest cultural scenes in the nation, centered on the area around Elm Street and what is now Central Expressway, which was then the railroad track for the Houston & Texas Central Railway. Known as "Deep Ellum," the area hosted a rich cultural mix, with pawnshops owned by Eastern European Jews next door to black-owned barber shops, theaters, and dance halls. "It is the one spot in the city that needs no daylight saving time because there is no bedtime, and working hours have no limits," wrote a black journalist. "The only place on earth where business, religion, hoodooism, gambling, and stealing go on at the same time without friction. . . ."[99]

Deep Ellum was especially famous for the blues artists that found their voice there. The best known was probably Blind Lemon Jefferson, who by the time of his death in 1929 was the best-selling African American blues singer in the country. Other important Deep Ellum blues performers were Huddie "Leadbelly" Ledbetter, Lonnie Johnson, and Little Hat Jones. Deep Ellum was

Deep Ellum, on the edge of downtown Dallas, was the site of a lively mixture of pawn shops, theaters, and street musicians during the 1920s. *Courtesy Dallas Public Library.*

also a regular stop for touring blues and jazz performers such as Bessie Smith and Ma Rainey.[100]

The city's cultural life in general thrived during the 1920s. The Dallas Symphony Orchestra, which had struggled as a part-amateur group since 1900, was reorganized in 1925 under the direction of Paul Van Katwijk, dean of music at Southern Methodist University. The Dallas Little Theater won New York's Belasco Cup three years running in the mid-1920s, and several local artists founded the Art Institute of Dallas.[101] Vaudeville and movie theaters lined Elm Street. Dallas was on the cutting edge of new entertainment technology with two radio stations—WRR, which in 1921 became the first municipally owned station in the country to feature scheduled entertainment programs, and WFAA, founded in 1922 as "a radio service of the Dallas *Morning News*," which quickly became a local institution with such programs as "The Early Birds."[102]

During the 1920s Dallasites became used to greeting celebrities from Hollywood and New York, who would arrive at Union Station or step out of a limousine in front of the Majestic Theater to the flash of cameras. Metropolitan Opera singer Leonora Corona (stage name of Dallas native Lenore Cohran), for example, gave several homecoming recitals in Dallas in the twenties.[103] But the visit of Charles Lindbergh in 1927 set records. Having captured the world's imagination with his solo flight across the Atlantic, Lindbergh was on a national tour when he reached Dallas on a rainy September afternoon. Some 10,000 spectators greeted him at the airport, and then he was escorted on a parade through downtown witnessed by the largest crowd in the city's history, estimated at 100,000 people. In the crowd were 40,000 school children who had been dismissed from school just to see the famed aviator.

At a banquet that evening, Lindbergh advised Dallasites: "Keep your airport—it will place you among the commercial leaders of the world."[104] The airport to which Lindbergh referred, Love Field, south of Bachman Lake, had actually been founded by the U.S. Army in 1917 as a flying school. After the war, the Dallas Chamber of Commerce took over the field and operated it aggressively, winning airmail service in 1926 and inaugurating the state's

In this 1929 photograph, a Fokker tri-motor airplane stands in front of the first terminal building at Love Field. *Courtesy Dallas Public Library.*

first commercial passenger flight in 1927. At the time of Lindbergh's visit, the city was negotiating to buy the field, which was accomplished after a bond election in December. Without a navigable river, Dallas had focused on the railroads as the city's transportation link with the world. Now the city would pursue the benefits of air transport.[105]

The city's skyline was also reaching new heights. When the twenty-nine-story Magnolia Building was completed in 1921, it was the tallest building west of the Mississippi River, a record it held until World War II. Downtown streets were becoming urban canyons, lined with multi-storied banks and office buildings. In 1934, in honor of the convention of the American Petroleum Institute, the "flying red horse" (Pegasus) was installed on top of the Magnolia Building. It was the world's largest revolving sign, lit at night with neon so that it was visible for miles. The winged horse of the Greek Muses, a symbol of hope, Pegasus quickly became an emblem for Dallas.

By 1934, Dallas residents needed something to lift their spirits. The Great Depression which hit the nation at the end of 1929 had put 18,500 Dallasites out of work by 1931. An emergency relief committee appointed by the Chamber of Commerce requested $100,000 to relieve hunger and poverty in Dallas. The city undertook a number of building projects to create jobs, including viaducts over the Trinity River and the land reclaimed by the levee project. Following the inauguration of Franklin D. Roosevelt in 1933, Dallas participated in many of the national recovery programs; for example, Public Works Administration funds helped re-employ nearly 11,000 persons that year.[106] Attempts to unionize workers met with only limited success; in the case of women garment workers, police responded to strikers with violence.[107]

Dallas benefited from the discovery of oil in East Texas in 1930, although not a drop of the black gold was ever discovered in Dallas County itself. Oil producers, investors, promoters, contractors, and corporations all found Dallas a convenient location for their headquarters. Twenty-eight oil-related companies located in Dallas during the first two months of 1931 alone. Sympathetic bankers, willing to consider underground oil reserves as collateral, profited, as did home builders, real estate agents, fashionable stores like Neiman-Marcus, and others ready to serve the newly rich oil tycoons. By 1941, 18 to 20 percent of those in the Dallas area depended on the oil industry for their income.[108]

The same entrepreneurial spirit that prompted Dallas civic leaders to pursue the benefits of aviation and oil for their city also motivated them to bid for the Texas Centennial Exposition, scheduled for 1936. San Antonio (site of the Alamo) and Houston (near San Jacinto) both had strong historic claims to host the celebration of Texas's independence from Mexico. Dallas, of course, had not even existed in 1836. But, as with the railroads in the 1870s and the Federal Reserve Bank in 1914, Dallas leaders were not about to let this opportunity pass them by.

Leading the effort to procure the Centennial Exposition was a man who would eventually be known as "Mr. Dallas," Robert L. Thornton. Born in a half-sod dugout in Central Texas, Thornton had grown up picking cotton on a farm in Ellis County. Early jobs as a road builder, store clerk, and candy salesman eventually led to a partnership in a small Dallas bank. By the mid-1930s, Thornton was head of one of the "big three" banks in Dallas, the Mercantile.[109] He persuaded his civic colleagues and the city council that the Centennial would provide a terrific economic boost to the city, and that to lose it could also jeopardize the State Fair. Under his leadership, the city put together a proposal that not only was the most financially appealing—$7,791,000—but was also the best organized and attractive. Dallas was awarded the Centennial in September 1934.[110]

During the next year and a half, under the general supervision of architect George Dahl, Fair Park was expanded and completely transformed. Hundreds of workmen, including artists and craftsmen, were put to work constructing or remodeling seventy-seven buildings, many of them designed to be permanent additions, such as the Hall of State, the Museum of Fine Arts, and the Museum of Natural History. The overall architectural design was "Art Deco," inspired by the 1925 Exposition des Arts Decoratifs in Paris.[111]

More than 250,000 people lined the streets to watch the inaugural parade on June 6, 1936. Six days later President Roosevelt visited

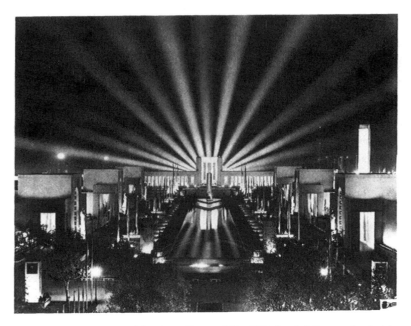

The Art Deco splendor of the Texas Centennial in 1936 dazzled thousands of visitors to Dallas. *Courtesy Dallas Historical Society.*

the grounds. Inside were theatrical shows, music, a carnival midway, a midget village, and an ice-skating show. An outdoor theater hosted a historical pageant called "The Cavalcade of Texas," complete with cowboys, Indians, and horses. Corporations such as General Motors showcased their products; the National Cash Register Company erected a pavilion shaped like a cash register, with the daily attendance figures appearing in the register's window at the top. Texas Centennial "Rangerettes" welcomed visitors, many of whom returned again and again to witness the wonders of what was essentially a World's Fair.

Nineteen thirty-six has been called "the year America discovered Texas."[112] Visitors came from every state and from throughout the world—more than six million people in six months. Hotel business was up 35 percent, restaurant sales grew by 50 percent, and wholesale sales increased as much as 40 percent.[113] The public relations value to Dallas was beyond measure. Suddenly, Dallas was "news," and not as a provincial, western town, but as a sophisticated, modern metropolis. The city was so pleased with the results that it staged the whole event again the next year, calling it the Greater Texas and Pan American Exposition.

Not all groups in Dallas had been allowed to participate fully in the Centennial. The organizers had offered to support a state appropriation for an African American exhibit only if a black candidate for the state legislature would withdraw from the race. When he refused, the planners blocked the appropriation, and it was only with Federal assistance that the Hall of Negro Life was built at the fairgrounds. Even then, Centennial officials planted large shrubs that obscured the building from casual passers-by. As soon as the Centennial was over, the planners of the Pan American Exposition had the Hall torn down, claiming it did not fit the theme; it was the only major structure so treated.[114]

However, African Americans had begun to organize politically through the Progressive Voters League, and in the 1937 municipal elections their influence had been sufficient to win promises of a new black high school (Lincoln), a new recreation center, and an increase in employment of African Americans by the city. Another demand, for black police officers, proved too controversial for the white power structure and was not fulfilled until after World War II.[115] Finding adequate housing in Dallas was also a growing problem for African Americans, and attempts in 1940 and 1941 to move into formerly white neighborhoods were met with bombings, mysterious fires, and stone and rock throwing.

The status of Mexican Americans in Dallas was not much better. In Little Mexico, the principal barrio just north of downtown, none of the streets were paved, nobody had hot water, and three-fourths of the residents lived without gas heating or indoor plumbing. Almost 60 percent of the residents lived without electricity. A 1935 study concluded that 74 percent of the houses were overcrowded, and 40 percent were "unfit for occupancy." Inevitably, contagious disease was rampant. Between 1934 and 1936, Little Mexico had the highest death rate in Dallas from tuberculosis.[116]

World War II masked some of the problems, as many minority males entered the armed forces, while factories such as the Ford Motor plant converted to wartime production and began hiring women. The new North American Aviation plant in the suburb of Grand Prairie employed 30,000 workers who built B-24 bombers, P-51 Mustangs, and AT-6 Texan trainers.[117]

Although much energy was focused on the war effort, Dallas began to ready itself for the future by commissioning Harland Bartholomew of St. Louis to develop a new master plan for the city. Published in 1943, Bartholomew's plan stressed the importance of careful zoning, advocated canalization of the Trinity, and reiterated Kessler's suggestion that a "Central Boulevard" replace the Houston & Texas Central railroad tracks.

Dallas had survived the trauma of the Ku Klux Klan in the 1920s to enjoy the triumph of the 1936 Centennial. Civic leaders intended to insure that the postwar era added new laurels to Dallas's reputation as a city that worked.

5.
DYNAMISM
AND DISASTER

THE SUCCESS OF THE 1936 Centennial was due primarily to the fact that R. L. Thornton had put together a 100-man committee composed of local board chairmen and company presidents to sponsor the event. He said he wanted "yes" men, men who could commit their company's funds without approval by anybody else. Once the Centennial was over, Thornton decided there was merit in keeping the group alive. At first he wanted to call it the "yes or no" council, but the more dignified name "Dallas Citizens Council" was finally chosen.

Membership on the council was by invitation only. To be eligible, one had to be the chief executive officer or president or the top executive of a firm doing business in Dallas. This included especially the city's leading bankers, insurance men, manufacturers, merchants, and the publishers of the daily newspapers. It largely excluded professional people such as lawyers, doctors, and teachers, as well as labor leaders. The inclusion of the newspaper publishers into the inner circle—and their willingness to join it— meant that the city's media would generally support projects or goals backed by the council.[118]

The Dallas Citizens Council wanted to promote ordered growth for the city, making it a place attractive to businessmen and investors. While it had no official powers, the group exercised far more influence over municipal and civic affairs than the elected city council, but without publicity. Working quietly behind the scenes, the DCC, with bankers always prominent, put its money and muscle behind the projects it considered important for the city. In the postwar era it supported projects like improvements at Love Field, canalization of the Trinity River to encourage barge traffic and shipping, improvements to the State Fair grounds, and a downtown auditorium.[119]

The unofficial political arm of the DCC was the Citizens Charter Association, a group originally formed to promote adoption of the council-manager form of municipal government in 1930. Convinced that Dallas should be run like an efficient corporation, the CCA advocated hiring a professional city manager to supervise the operations of the city. He would report to a city council composed of nonpartisan business leaders, who would set policy much like a board of directors, but who would maintain a "hands off" attitude toward daily administration.

Once the council-manager system was in place, the CCA remained in existence to make sure "the right type of men" were elected to the city council. It became a sort of political party on the local level, selecting candidates, financing their campaigns, and rallying public support. Although the CCA's membership was fairly broad, including many small businessmen and others, its leadership was tightly controlled—overlapping often with that of the Citizens Council after 1937—and it was this elite that selected candidates and made key policy decisions.

Although the CCA lost seats on the council in 1935 and 1937, it regained control in 1939, and during World War II its candidates frequently ran unopposed. The two daily newspapers always gave the CCA strong support. "The issue is whether we shall have a united, harmonious governing body at city hall, or one composed of two warring factions," observed the Dallas Morning News in 1947.[120]

In the interest of maintaining the image of a harmonious city government, the CCA proved adept at accommodating challengers. When council member J. B. Adoue led a campaign to change the city charter to allow direct election of the mayor (who had formerly been elected by the council members from among

R. L. Thornton (center) and former Dallas mayors celebrated the "completion" of Central Expressway in 1956. Occupying the former right-of-way of the Houston & Texas Central Railway, the expressway was in fact far from complete. *Courtesy Dallas Historical Society.*

themselves), the CCA supported the campaign and even endorsed Adoue for mayor in 1951. But after a chaotic two years in which Adoue tried to fire the city manager and publicly criticized the police department, the CCA persuaded the venerable R. L. Thornton to run for mayor. In 1953 the CCA nominated (and elected) Bill Harris, president of the local chapter of the AFL, for the council, and in 1957 it brought Calvert Collins onto the council as its first woman member.

During his nine years as mayor, Thornton presided over a city council whose members had no offices in city hall, no personal staff support, and only token pay. The CCA had always prided itself on giving Dallas corruption-free government, and this claim was remarkably true. "With the city's steady record of economic growth and progress for so many decades, CCA and Citizen Council leaders had no temptation to add to their well-being through corruption," one historian has observed. "They were making plenty of money honestly through free enterprise."[121]

During Mayor Thornton's administration (1953–1961), the city fulfilled his mandate to "keep the dirt flying" by embarking on a host of construction projects. A new public library opened in 1955, replacing the old Carnegie Library, and work began on a new addition to city hall. The Dallas Convention Center and Memorial Auditorium were dedicated in 1957, and a six-lane toll road between Dallas and Fort Worth opened the same year. Private developers began construction of the Dallas Market Center in 1955, a complex that eventually grew to include the Trade Mart, Market Hall, Apparel Mart, Decorative Center, World Trade Center, and the Infomart—the world's largest single-site market complex.

The postwar period saw the rise of the so-called "Sunbelt," as well-educated middle class professionals flocked to the South and Southwest to pursue good-paying jobs in new, "clean" industries such as aviation and electronics.[122] With its geographic centrality, modern airport, and strong free-enterprise climate, Dallas was among the fastest growing of the Sunbelt cities. From a population of less than 300,000 in 1940, Dallas exploded to nearly 435,000 by 1950 and 680,000 by 1960. Its land mass nearly doubled to 90 square miles after the war, and small county towns like Garland, Richardson, and Mesquite became commuter suburbs. Between 1945 and 1955, Dallas created 151,000 new jobs and built 105,000 dwelling units, 350 churches, 36 schools, and 25 major office buildings. As a result, the tax valuation increased more than $700 million. No wonder the Dallas *Times Herald* referred to these years as the "Dynamic Decade."[123]

Not all segments of Dallas participated equally in the prosperity of the 1950s. During the post–World War II period, thousands of African Americans moved to Dallas from small towns and rural areas seeking a better life. The 1950 Federal Census listed the number of nonwhites (principally blacks, since Mexican Americans were numbered with whites) as 83,352, or 13.5 percent of the total population. The city still had done little to alleviate the housing shortage for black families, except for building some public housing units for the poorest. At the same time, the construction of

Central Expressway in the late 1940s destroyed blocks of African American houses and cut a barrier right through the middle of the historic State-Thomas neighborhood, Dallas's original post–Civil War Freedmen's Town.

As African Americans began buying houses in fringe areas of South Dallas, they were again greeted with bombings. After half a dozen black homes were destroyed, police began to patrol the neighborhood more vigilantly, but their presence didn't seem to stop the bombings. Small "scare" bombs were tossed at black women walking along the sidewalks. The bombings, which were clearly designed to intimidate African Americans and discourage them from buying houses in the area, persisted over a two-year period and became the subject of national publicity.[124]

Concerned about the poor image being projected of Dallas at a time when the economy was really starting to boom and companies were beginning to be attracted to Dallas, the leadership of the Dallas Citizens Council persuaded the district attorney to empanel a special grand jury, composed of leading citizens including three African Americans, to investigate the bombings. Although the investigations began to point to some prominent white citizens, the grand jury adjourned without indicting any of the major players, convinced that they would never be convicted in a courtroom. And indeed, the only man who was ever brought to trial, a man against whom eyewitness testimony seemed overwhelming, was found not guilty by a white jury.[125] The bombings, however, did stop. And a group of white civic leaders took the initiative to design and build a middle-class African American residential neighborhood called Hamilton Park in what was then far north Dallas, near the intersection of what is today Central Expressway and LBJ Freeway.

The Supreme Court's *Brown vs. Board of Education* decision in May 1954, which declared segregation unconstitutional in the public schools, is widely recognized as a watershed event in pulling down racial barriers in the United States. In September 1954 the Reverend R. C. McNeil and thirty-two black parents filed a petition to end school segregation in Dallas. The Dallas School Board delayed integration for nearly a decade, beginning a "stairstep" plan in 1961, whereby one grade a year would be integrated. This was declared inadequate four years later. Junior high schools were finally desegregated in 1966, and high schools the following year. But not until 1994 did a federal judge declare the Dallas Independent School District officially desegregated.[126]

Desegregation of public facilities such as restaurants and stores proceeded without violence once the white power structure finally realized it had to happen. A "Committee of 14," composed of seven of the most powerful white civic leaders in Dallas and seven prominent African Americans, was charged with negotiating the desegregation of public facilities throughout Dallas. One of their strategies was the production of a film to sell the idea of peaceful desegregation to the community. Narrated by Walter Cronkite, the thirty-minute film, entitled "Dallas at the Crossroads," showed only white people and preached nonviolence and the necessity of accepting the law in order to maintain the good national image of the city. Most downtown stores desegregated in 1962; city parks, swimming pools, and theaters were desegregated in 1963; the State Fair ended "Negro Achievement Day" in 1967; and several African Americans were appointed to city boards and commissions.[127]

While the civic leadership was being forced by the federal courts to be more inclusive of racial minorities, it was also facing challenges from some of the new middle-class professionals who had recently moved to Dallas. Without historic ties to the city, many were more interested in their careers and neighborhoods than in "the city as a whole," which often translated into "the central business district." In 1954 Bruce Alger, a real estate salesman who had been active in the White Rock Chamber of Commerce, ran for Congress against Wallace Savage, a former mayor. An aggressive campaigner, Alger tied himself to the coattails of popular Republican President Dwight Eisenhower and won the race. Alger became one of the most conservative members of the U.S. Congress, denouncing the United Nations, "creeping communism," and free-lunch programs for children. He consistently voted against federal funding programs, even those that might benefit Dallas. Yet Alger enjoyed a strong base of support in his east Dallas constituency and was regularly re-elected, much to the chagrin of the old-guard Dallas leadership.[128]

The brand of rabid anti-communism espoused by Alger led to several embarrassing incidents in Dallas during the 1950s. A group calling itself the Dallas Patriotic Council attacked the Museum of Fine Arts for a touring exhibit, "Sport in Art," which included works by several artists whom the council accused of being communists or communist sympathizers.[129] Although the trustees of the art museum stood firm against censorship on political grounds, the director of the public library agreed to remove works by Pablo Picasso from a special exhibition when similar attacks were levied against him.[130]

By the early 1960s Dallas had become a hotbed of political ultraconservatism. A number of ugly incidents enforced the city's image as a haven of right wing fanatics. When Lyndon and Lady Bird Johnson were in Dallas during the 1960 presidential campaign, they were taunted and spat upon by a mob as they crossed Commerce Street from one hotel to another. Retired Army General Edwin Walker, active in the John Birch Society, flew the American flag upside down at his house as a distress signal that the nation was in danger of being taken over by the communists. At a White House luncheon Ted Dealey, publisher of the Dallas *Morning News*, rudely lectured President Kennedy, telling him America needed a strong president who would get off Caroline's tricycle and lead the nation from horseback. In October 1963, as he was getting into his car following a speech at Memorial Auditorium, Adlai Stevenson, ambassador to the United Nations, was struck over the head by a placard carried by a woman in the crowd.

So when President Kennedy announced plans to visit Dallas in November 1963, there were concerns about the reception he would receive, and suggestions by some of his aides that he skip Dallas. He decided to come anyway. Handbills were circulated throughout the city bearing pictures of President Kennedy with the words "Wanted for Treason." A full-page advertisement appeared in the *Morning News*, surrounded by black borders, asking the president accusatory questions. Yet the crowds that met him at the airport and that lined the streets of his motorcade were

The Dallas *Times Herald* remade its afternoon edition to report the assassination of President John F. Kennedy. *Courtesy A. H. Belo Corporation Archives.*

cheering and enthusiastic. Only at the end, as the limousines turned down Elm Street at Dealey Plaza, were the shots fired that killed the president and wounded Texas Governor John Connally.

Dallasites were as shocked and saddened by the assassination as the rest of the nation. Some were privately relieved when the man arrested for the crime, Lee Harvey Oswald, turned out not to be a right-wing zealot, as might have been expected, but a Marxist who had spent time in the Soviet Union.[131] Then, less than forty-eight hours after the president's assassination, Oswald was shot and killed in front of television cameras as he was being escorted through the basement of the police station to be transfered to the county jail.

Dallas was labeled "the city of hate." The mayor's office was deluged with angry letters from around the country, and harsh long-distance telephone calls flooded the police station. Dallasites traveling in other cities often found themselves subject to rudeness. Although many in the city reacted with defensiveness—an "it could have happened anywhere" attitude—others, such as Stanley Marcus, called for Dallas to adopt a new, more tolerant mood, rejecting extremism and encouraging moderation.[132]

One thing was clear to the leadership: Bruce Alger would have to go. Mayor Earle Cabell, then in his second term, resigned to run against Alger in the November 1964 elections and won. Under the city charter, a majority of the city council was to appoint a successor to the mayor. The six CCA council members, along with the president of the Dallas Citizens Council, John Stemmons, met privately and asked J. Erik Jonsson to step in. Jonsson was a wealthy, self-made industrialist who had played a key role in transforming Texas Instruments into a worldwide firm on the cutting edge of technology. Jonsson was known as a visionary, good at planning and goal setting. As soon as Cabell resigned, the council elected Jonsson mayor, despite protests by the non-CCA, independent council members that they had been excluded from the deliberations. "This may be a benevolent oligarcy," one of them complained, "but it isn't representative government."[133]

Nevertheless, Erik Jonsson was to be one of Dallas's great mayors, the man who more than any other helped the city recover from the stigma of the Kennedy assassination.

6.
DIVERSITY
AND DEMOCRACY

ERIK JONSSON SERVED as mayor of Dallas from 1964 until 1970, considerably longer than the fifteen months he had originally envisioned. He was to be the last CCA mayor and in some ways the most successful, at least in creating an image of a modern, efficient, well-run city government that worked to unite the citizens. A particularly successful project Jonsson initiated, in late 1964, was called Goals for Dallas. He asked citizens to help come up with common goals for such areas as local government, transportation, health and welfare, education, cultural activities, and recreation. A permanent office was set up, and meetings were held throughout the city. As priorities began to emerge, a series of books was published describing them and setting deadlines. Voters passed a bond proposal in 1967 to construct a new city hall and adjoining park plaza, and another bond proposal two years later to air-condition public schools and implement a kindergarten program. Goals for Dallas continued as an ongoing project and probably played a role in getting Dallas named in 1970 an "all-American city" by *Look* magazine, the only city in its size category to be so honored.[134]

Erik Jonsson was also the key player in persuading Dallas and Fort Worth to cooperate in building a regional airport. Since the 1930s, the two cities had feuded over the airport, Dallas wanting to preserve the convenient and profitable Love Field, Fort Worth wanting a regional airport equidistant from the two cities. Love Field was a source of great community pride, and Dallas had continued to pour money into upgrading its facilities, despite the fact that it was hemmed in on all sides by residential and commercial development that precluded any expansion. In 1964 the Civil Aeronautics Board issued an ultimatum: Dallas and Fort Worth had six months to agree on a site for a regional airport; otherwise, the CAB would designate one for them. Jonsson initiated discussions with Fort Worth officials, and by 1965 both city councils had agreed to create a regional airport authority to build and operate a facility at a site midway between the two cities.[135] Dallas–Fort Worth International Airport opened in 1974 and soon became the second busiest in the nation.

Another of Jonsson's decisions proved to be less farsighted. Since its organization in 1960, the Dallas Cowboys had developed rapidly into one of the nation's premier professional football franchises. However, the aging Cotton Bowl at Fair Park, where the Cowboys played their home games, was inadequate, and the team's owner, Clint Murchison Jr., began exploring options to build a downtown stadium. Jonsson nixed the idea, and so the Cowboys built a new stadium in the Dallas suburb of Irving.[136] In 1972, the year after Texas Stadium opened, the Cowboys won their first Super Bowl victory.

During Jonsson's term as mayor, the composition of the city council and the way in which council members were chosen began to undergo some significant changes. Ever since the council-manager form of government had been adopted in 1930, the Dallas City Council had consisted of nine members, six of whom represented specific districts, but all of whom were elected at large. The six district representatives didn't even have to reside in their districts.

In the 1967 elections, the CCA candidate for the Pleasant Grove area, Jesse Price, was elected over an independent rival, Max Goldblatt, who operated a hardware store in the area. Price won the seat because of his city-wide majority, but Goldblatt had actually won the majority of votes within Pleasant Grove, the district the seat was supposed to represent. Goldblatt filed suit in federal court to change the system so that residents from individual districts could elect their own council members.

By the time three judges heard Goldblatt's case in 1968, Dallas voters had already approved a charter amendment expanding the council's size from nine to eleven members and establishing residency requirements for the first time. Now, eight of the eleven council members had to live in designated districts. But they would all still be elected by city-wide vote.

Proponents of at-large voting argued that, as long as the members were elected city-wide, they could resist narrow, parochial pressures and consider what was best for the city as a whole. The counter argument was that because voter turnout was much higher in the wealthier northern sections of the city, they tended to have a disproportionate influence on the council, and thus received a disproportionate share of city services. Only when residents in the eastern, southern, and western portions of the city elected their own council members would they begin to get their fair share of city services.

One immediate effect of the enlargement of the city council was that the CCA appointed George L. Allen, a distinguished black businessman who had already twice run unsuccessfully for the council, to fill the place for District 8, which represented South Dallas. Allen followed C. A. Galloway, another African American who had been appointed to fill out two weeks remaining in a term for the Pleasant Grove seat soon contested by Goldblatt. But Allen was the first black to serve a meaningful term on the council.[137] In 1969 the council gained its first Mexican American member, Anita Martinez, whom the CCA endorsed for one of the at-large seats.

Erik Jonsson's retirement in 1970 opened the door to a free-for-all mayoral race that ended with the election of an independent, Wes Wise, a councilman who had been a sportscaster on Dallas radio and television. The CCA lost two other council seats. Concerned about its future, the CCA commissioned a poll to assess its image in the community. The results indicated that the CCA must broaden its base of support if it hoped to continue as a major political force. The city was much more diverse than it used to be. The report concluded, "Today there is no longer the possibility of the business community alone guiding and directing the growth of the city."[138]

In the next elections, the CCA did not seriously oppose Mayor Wise, and it added a black woman, Lucy Patterson, to its slate, along with George Allen, Adlene Harrison (a Jewish woman), and Pedro Aguirre to replace Anita Martinez. After the elections, George Allen was elected mayor pro tem, the first minority to hold a leadership position. Meanwhile, a group of minority activists filed a lawsuit challenging the at-large election system. On January 17, 1975, Federal Judge Eldon Mahon declared Dallas's at-large system of voting unconstitutional. The system, he said, "diluted" minority voting strength, gave undue power to white-dominated groups "such as the Citizens Charter Association," and made the cost of running a city-wide race prohibitive. The judge ordered the city to draw up a new plan for the upcoming April election.[139] The council quickly devised an 8-3 scheme, which the judge approved, in which eight council members would be elected from specific single-member districts, while the mayor and two at-large candidates would be elected city-wide.

The CCA had already been split trying to find a good candidate to run against Mayor Wise. In the election, Wise trounced his CCA opponent, two incumbent CCA candidates were defeated, and the CCA held on to just six seats. Then George Allen, the CCA's first black candidate, resigned to take a justice of the peace appointment and was replaced by Juanita Craft, a distinguished seventy-three-year-old NAACP organizer, who was most definitely an independent. For the first time since the 1930s, the CCA found itself with a minority of the council seats.

By the end of 1975 the Citizens Charter Association had virtually collapsed, the victim of a gradual but dramatic change in Dallas. The 1970s were an era when citizens everywhere were speaking out and demanding a greater share in government. In Dallas, a host of new organizations appeared, representing neighborhoods, minorities, historic preservationists, supporters of the arts, etc. The newspapers had opened up greatly, thanks in part to the impact of television and investigative reporting. Conflicting ideas and ideologies were given a hearing, and even a legitimacy, they had

Dallas's new City Hall, designed by I. M. Pei, opened in 1978. *Photograph by the author.*

never enjoyed before. As one historian put it, "no longer could traditional downtown Dallas businessmen control the city's destiny through decisions made at a luncheon."[140]

Nevertheless, the city was prospering as it had not since the 1950s. The economy boomed as oil prices climbed and corporations such as American Airlines, J. C. Penney, and Exxon relocated their headquarters to the area. Continued migration to the Sunbelt boosted Dallas's population to 904,078 by 1980, making it the seventh-largest city in the nation. Geographically, Dallas expanded its boundaries to encompass 378 square miles, pushing beyond the limits of Dallas County for the first time. In 1978 CBS premiered a new weekly series called "Dallas," which reinforced an international image of the city as a glitzy, hustling metropolis. That same year, an ultra-modern city hall, designed by I. M. Pei, opened on a broad plaza adjacent to the expanding convention center. In 1982 a new central library opened across the street. The Dallas Museum of Art occupied its new facility downtown in 1984, and the symphony orchestra moved into the Pei-designed Meyerson Symphony Hall in 1989. The opening of The Sixth Floor Museum in the former Texas School Book Depository Building in 1989 helped resolve some of the city's lingering guilt over its role in President Kennedy's assassination.[141]

Private development outpaced even these public projects. New downtown skyscrapers left the Magnolia Building and its flying red horse in the shadows. Ever-larger, air-conditioned shopping malls dotted the suburban landscape, as new residential communities spread across what had once been farmland. As Dallas lost much of its architectural heritage to the wrecking ball, historic preservationists succeeded in reviving the West End warehouse district on the edge of downtown with restaurants and shops, and in transforming Deep Ellum into an eclectic mix of galleries, clubs, and dining spots.

In 1987 Dallas voters elected their first woman mayor, Annette Strauss, a longtime community volunteer.[142] She defeated an establishment male who had been endorsed by four former mayors. Although she herself was a wealthy north Dallasite, the sister-in-law of Democratic Party stalwart Bob Strauss, her election was seen as another sign of changing times at city hall.

Mrs. Strauss had to preside over a local economy hit hard by the recession of the late 1980s, when the price of oil plummeted and the savings-and-loan industry collapsed. Property values began to decline, exacerbated by "white flight" to the suburbs as the Dallas Independent School District continued to struggle with court-ordered desegregation. The city's tax base declined, limiting the services the city could afford to offer. Residents began to complain about deteriorating streets, parks, and garbage collection. Immigrants from Southeast Asia and the Pacific Islands were making Dallas more cosmopolitan and diverse. Yet there was also a continuing heated debate over police-minority relationships, fueled by several incidents in which minorities felt they had been unfairly targeted by Dallas police.

When Mayor Strauss appointed a blue-ribbon panel to recommend ways to promote racial harmony in the city, one of its conclusions was that the 8-3 council system did not provide adequate representation for all citizens. Strauss therefore appointed a special Charter Review Commission, which eventually came up with what was called the 10-4-1 plan. This would have expanded the number of single-member districts from eight to ten, and also had four members from large quadrants, with the mayor elected by everybody. Some of the minority members on the commission accepted this, but others denounced it, wanting a plan by which all the members except the mayor would be elected from specific districts.

Despite angry protesters in the council chambers, the city council voted in June 1989 to submit the 10-4-1 plan to the voters. In August Dallas approved it by a two-thirds majority. However, there were sharp divisions along racial lines. While 85 percent of white voters voted for the plan, 95 percent of African Americans opposed it, as did 70 percent of Hispanics.

Meanwhile two African Americans, Marvin Crenshaw and Roy Williams, had filed a federal lawsuit, arguing that the old 8-3 council plan was unconstitutional. In March 1990, U.S. District Judge Jerry Buchmeyer agreed. Although he did not rule specifically on the 10-4-1 plan, his comments indicated that it too might not meet his criteria. The city council, hoping to settle the issue, then submitted a 14-1 plan with single-member districts to the voters. In one of the highest turnouts ever for a city charter referendum, voters rejected it by a narrow 372 votes. However, Judge Buchmeyer ordered a council election on the 14-1 plan. Because of the two public referendums, the city felt obligated to appeal his decision and submitted the 10-4-1 plan to the U.S. Justice Department for approval. In May the Justice Department agreed with Judge Buchmeyer that the 10-4-1 plan was inadequate. At this point, the city yielded, having spent more than $1 million in legal fees to support the 10-4-1 plan, and agreed to adopt the 14-1 plan.

So, after a bitter fight, how the council would be elected had been decided. Now the challenge was to draw the new district lines in such a way as to accomplish the ultimate goal, which was to increase minority representation on the council. Tempers ran high as council members debated how to divide Oak Cliff, Pleasant Grove, and other neighborhoods. Ironically, the fact that blacks in

Dallas had for so long been subject to discriminatory housing patterns and still tended to live in more concentrated geographic areas made it somewhat easier to draw boundaries that would increase the likelihood of an African American being elected. Because Mexican Americans were more dispersed through the city, it was harder to draw districts that benefited them. When finally agreed on, the borders of the fourteen new districts zigzagged up and down city streets, making odd, surprising turns, as they located appropriate racial mixes.[143]

When elected in 1993, the new city council was remarkably diverse. It included the conservative Republican Mayor Steve Bartlett, two Mexican Americans who differed rather markedly in their goals and approaches, a black woman from West Dallas, and a bearded white liberal who had presided over a city-wide home-owners' group. All told, there were nine whites, four blacks, and two Hispanics.

This new council was much more political than any before it. Council members—still receiving only token pay despite filling nearly full-time posts—quickly became frustrated at their inability to deal directly with city departments on behalf of their constituents. Ironically, in both 1992 and 1993 the magazine *Financial World* declared Dallas to be the best-managed city in the nation for handling its resources.[144] Nevertheless, after several acrimonious months, Jan Hart, the city manager, resigned in October 1993 to become an investment banker. The council quickly appointed the first assistant city manager, John Ware, an African American, to succeed her. In the 1995 council elections, voters chose Ron Kirk, an African American, as mayor. Under his leadership, the council coalesced to work in a less strident tone to deal with the city's business.

In the past thirty years, Dallas has replaced a nonpartisan municipal government, tightly controlled by a business elite, with a democratic form responsive to the diverse constituencies that make up the modern city. Yet the goal of that government remains essentially the same: to provide a stable, encouraging climate for economic growth through which the more than one million citizens of Dallas can enjoy prosperous, productive lives.

CONCLUSION

IN THE LAST HALF CENTURY, a popular myth has arisen that Dallas is an "accidental" city, one with no obvious reason for being. Not located on a navigable waterway, it became a transportation center only through the determination of its civic leaders. Likewise, its regional dominance in banking, insurance, publishing, and other industries was the achievement of single-minded businessmen and women. "People made Dallas," goes the myth, "visionary, hard-working individuals."

While such a myth is attractive ("We accomplished it all by ourselves, with no help from nature!"), it should be clear from the foregoing that Dallas's location, its natural resources, and even its climate have all played key roles in its development. John Neely Bryan chose the site because it was adjacent to one of the best fords across the Trinity River for miles around. Early settlers were attracted by the fertile terrain. The sunny, relatively dry climate became increasingly attractive to residents of the eastern and northern United States as the twentieth century progressed.

The history of Dallas is really a story about how individuals capitalized on the city's natural assets, especially its geographic centrality in a rapidly developing transportation network, to create a major city. At the same time, they had to deal with the conflicts and challenges that inevitably arose in a fast-growing city with an increasingly diverse population. For much of this century, tightly controlled,

Three eras in Dallas history: a pioneer log cabin, the Victorian "Old Red" court-house, and the modernistic Reunion Tower. *Photograph by the author.*

business-dominated civic leadership prevailed. In the past two decades, more democratic methods have slowly become dominant.

Dallas grew from a frontier market town to the nation's eighth-largest city in barely 150 years. As Dallas enters a new century, its residents will need to learn from that past—about how to agree on goals, how to identify and utilize assets, and how to resolve conflict. If they are successful, the next 150 years can be even more rewarding than the last.

NOTES

1. Brenda B. Whorton and William L. Young, "Before John Neely Bryan," *Legacies*, III (Fall, 1991), 4–10; Randall W. Moir, "Window to the Past," ibid., 11–16.

2. Edward Smith, *Account of a Journey Through North East Texas* (London: Hamilton, Adams & Co., 1848), 11–12.

3. Letter from Charles Barker, Dec. 1853, printed in David S. Switzer, *It's Our Dallas County* (Dallas: Switzer Educational Writings, 1954), 15.

4. Dallas Historical Society, A523; copy of broadside, dated June 1846, reproduced in Darwin Payne, *Dallas: An Illustrated History* (Woodland Hills, Calif.: Windsor Publications, 1982), 18.

5. A. C. Greene, "The Real Dallas Past," *Dallas Life* magazine in the Dallas *Morning News*, June 26, 1983; Payne, *Dallas: An Illustrated History*, 19–21.

6. "Memoirs of James J. Beeman (Written December 24, 1886)," typed manuscript (Dallas Historical Society). Bryan married Margaret Beeman, daughter of James's brother John, in 1843.

7. A. C. Greene, *A Place Called Dallas* (Dallas: Dallas County Heritage Society, 1975), 4.

8. Commodore Dallas is identified as the namesake by J. M. Morphis in his *History of Texas* (New York: United States Publishing Co., 1874), 516. See also A. C. Greene, "Dallas believed named for 1800s U.S. Navy hero," Dallas *Morning News*, Apr. 21, 1996.

9. Fannin County Deed Records, Book B, Aug. 27, 1842, p. 92, cited in Shirley Caldwell and Newton Fitzhugh, "The Making of a County: The 'Three Forks' Before 1846," *Heritage News*, XI (Winter, 1986–87), 13–17.

10. Houston *Morning Star*, Nov. 16, 1843, cited in John William Rogers, *The Lusty Texans of Dallas* (New York: E. P. Dutton, 1951), 43.

11. Smith, *Account of a Journey*, 14.

12. Mrs. George James, "Seventy Years in the Garland, Dallas County, Texas Area" (originally published as a series of articles in the Garland *News*, 1927).

13. John Beldon Billingsley, "A Trip to Texas," ed. Robert L. and Pauline Jones, *Texana*, VII (1969), 205.

14. F. E. Butterfield and C. M. Rundlett, *Directory of the City of Dallas . . . For the Year 1875* (1875; reprint, Dallas: Stone-Inge Books, 1979), 8.

15. Isaac Webb's diary (DeGolyer Library, Southern Methodist University, Dallas). Nancy Jane Cochran and Webb's wife, Mary, were sisters.

16. John Henry Brown, *History of Dallas County, Texas from 1837 to 1887* (1889; reprint, Dallas: Aldredge Book Store, 1966), 17. Mary Hord, Mary West, and other women taught children in their cabins before this; see Elizabeth York Enstam, "To Acquire a Little Book Learning," *Legacies*, VIII (Spring, 1996), 9.

17. Dallas County was almost certainly named for George Mifflin Dallas, Vice President of the United States since 1845.

18. J. M. Myers, "Recollections of Old Texians," Dallas *Sunday Mercury*, Mar. 18, 1883.

19. M. A. Col, "The Fulfillment!" trans. James W. Phillips (Dallas: DeGolyer Foundation Library, 1963), 1.

20. James Pratt, "Our European Heritage," *Legacies*, I (Fall, 1989), 14–17.

21. A. C. Greene, *A Town Called Cedar Springs* (Dallas: n.p., 1984), 24.

22. Butterfield and Rundlett, *Directory of the City of Dallas.*

23. Thomas H. Smith, "Blacks in Dallas: From Slavery to Freedom," *Heritage News*, X (Spring, 1975), 18–22.

24. Philip Lindsley, *A History of Greater Dallas and Vicinity* (2 vols.; Chicago: Lewis Publishing Co., 1909), I, 62–63.

25. Darwin Payne, "A Distressing and Fatal Rencontre," in *Sketches of a Growing Town*, ed. Darwin Payne (Dallas: Southern Methodist University, 1991), 22–35.

26. Elizabeth York Enstam, "The Reluctant Matriarch: Sarah Horton Cockrell," *D Magazine* (Mar., 1978), 82–83.

27. Payne, "A Distressing and Fatal Rencontre," 26.

28. Bryan fled Dallas in 1855 after shooting a man, whom Bryan mistakenly thought had died from the wound. Although Bryan must have learned fairly soon that the man survived, he did not return to his family in Dallas for nearly six years. Lucy C. Trent, *John Neely Bryan* (Dallas: Tardy, 1936).

29. Brown, *History of Dallas County, Texas*, 51.

30. W. S. Adair, "Dallas Was an Island in 1866," Dallas *Morning News*, Sept. 3, 1922, interview with Clifton Scott.

31. Quoted in Payne, *Dallas: An Illustrated History*, 46.

32. Dallas *Morning News*, Oct. 1, 1935, Part Three, Section VII.

33. Barrot Sanders, "Dallas to Galveston on the Mean Trinity," Dallas *Morning News*, Jan. 19, 1986 ("Texas 150," Sesquicentennial supplement, p. 15).

34. Smith, "Blacks in Dallas."

35. Cited in Payne, *Dallas: An Illustrated History*, 48.

36. Austin *State Gazette*, July 12, 1860; Houston *Telegraph and Texas Register*, July 12, 1860.

37. Maxine Holmes and Gerald D. Saxon (eds.), *The WPA Dallas Guide and History* (n.p.: Dallas Public Library, Texas Center for the Book, University of North Texas Press, 1992), 55.

38. Rogers, *The Lusty Texans of Dallas*, 99.

39. Lester Newton Fithugh (ed.), *Cannon Smoke: The Letters of Captain John J. Good, Good-Douglas Texas Battery, CSA* (Hillsboro: Hill Junior College Press, 1971), 78.

40. Thomas H. Smith, "Conflict and Corruption: The Dallas Establishment vs. the Freedmen's Bureau Agent," *Legacies*, I (Fall, 1989), 24–30.

41. Quoted in Payne, *Dallas: An Illustrated History*, 61.

42. John M. McCoy to his brother, Addie, Dec. 19, 1871, in *When Dallas Became a City*, ed. Elizabeth York Enstam (Dallas: Dallas Historical Society, 1982), 46.

43. Holmes and Saxon (eds.), *The WPA Dallas Guide* , 137.

44. While Lane introduced the bill into the Texas House, Samuel Evans introduced it in the Senate. A. C. Greene, "Pioneer town's location was close, but no cigar," Dallas *Morning News*, June 23, 1996.

45. Leon Rosenberg and Grant Davis, "Dallas and Its First Railroad," *Railroad History*, CXXXV (Fall, 1976), 38; Gerald D. Saxon (ed.), *Reminiscences: A Glimpse of Old East Dallas* (Dallas: Dallas Public Library, 1983), 9–10.

46. Dallas *Herald*, July 18, 1872. Bryan died in the State Lunatic Asylum in Austin on September 8, 1877.

47. John M. McCoy to his parents, July 7, 1872, in Enstam (ed.), *When Dallas Became a City*, 77.

48. Sam Acheson, *Dallas Yesterday* (Dallas: Southern Methodist University Press, 1977), 203–204.

49. Payne, *Dallas: An Illustrated History*, 63; A. C. Greene, *Dallas: The Deciding Years* (Austin: Encino Press, 1973), 21.

50. Holmes and Saxon (eds.), *The WPA Dallas Guide*, 139–140.

51. William McDonald, *Dallas Rediscovered* (Dallas: Dallas Historical Society, 1978), 21.

52. *Lawson & Edmondson's Dallas City Directory . . . for 1873–74* (Springfield: Missouri Patriot Book and Job Printing House, 1873), 11.

53. Leon Rosenberg, *Sangers: Pioneer Texas Merchants* (Austin: Texas State Historical Association, 1978).

54. Advertisements in the Dallas *Herald*, 1873 and 1874.

55. Among other accounts, see Rick Miller, *Bounty Hunter* (College Station: Creative Publishing Co., 1988), 33–78, and John Rogers, *The Lusty Texans of Dallas*, 140–154.

56. *Lawson & Edmondson's . . . Directory*, 99.

57 . Michael V. Hazel, "From Distant Shores: European Immigrants in Dallas," *Heritage News*, X (Spring, 1985), 9–15.

58. Ibid., 13–15.

59. Valentine J. Belfiglio, "Early Italian Settlers in Dallas: A New Life with Old

Values," *Heritage News*, X (Winter, 1985–1986), 4–7.

60. Interview with Nina Nixon-Mendez, Feb. 12, 1989; "Hispanic Beginnings of Dallas" exhibition, Old City Park, 1989; Gwendolyn Rice, "Little Mexico and the Barrios of Dallas," *Legacies*, IV (Fall, 1992), 21–27.

61. Jacquelyn M. McElhaney, "Childhood in Dallas, 1870–1900" (M.A. thesis, Southern Methodist University, 1982), 28–31.

62. Jackie McElhaney, "Dallas Public Schools: The First Decade," *Heritage News*, IX (Spring, 1984), 12–14; Rose-Mary Rumbley, *A Century of Class* (Austin: Eakin Press, 1984), 1–27.

63. Sam Acheson, *35,000 Days in Texas: A History of the Dallas News and Its Forbears* (New York: Macmillan Co., 1938), 98–108; Michael V. Hazel, "The Making of Two Modern Dailies," *Legacies*, IX (Spring, 1997), 4–14.

64. Both papers remained under local ownership until 1970, when the *Times Herald* was sold to the Times-Mirror Company. Several subsequent ownership changes weakened the paper, until it folded in December 1991, leaving Dallas with only one daily newspaper—the Dallas *Morning News*—for the first time since the 1870s.

65. Nancy Wiley, *The Great State Fair of Texas* (Dallas: Taylor Publishing Co., 1985).

66. Ibid., 35.

67. Jackie McElhaney, "Navigating the Trinity," *Legacies*, III (Spring, 1991), 7–8.

68. The population fell from 44,000 in 1892 to less than 39,000 in 1894. McDonald, *Dallas Rediscovered*, 70.

69. Carpenters successfully struck for a nine-hour working day in May 1890. Holmes and Saxon (eds.), *The WPA Dallas Guide*, 157.

70. Michael V. Hazel, "Dallas Women's Clubs: Vehicles for Change," *Heritage News*, XI (Spring, 1986), 18–21.

71. Jackie McElhaney, "The Only Clean, Bright Spot They Know," *Heritage News*, XI (Fall, 1986), 19–22.

72. Elizabeth York Enstam, "The Forgotten Frontier," *Legacies*, I (Spring, 1989), 20–28.

73. Jackie McElhaney, "Pauline Periwinkle: Crusading Columnist," *Heritage News*, X (Summer, 1985), 15–18.

74. Michael V. Hazel, "A Mother's Touch: The First Two Women Elected to the Dallas School Board," *Heritage News*, XII (Spring, 1987), 9–12.

75. Elizabeth York Enstam, unpublished manuscript on women in Dallas, 1840–1920.

76. Acheson, *35,000 Days in Texas*, 199–200.

77. Raymond A. Mohl, *The New City: Urban America in the Industrial Age, 1860–1920* (Arlington Heights, Ill.: Harlan Davidson, 1985), 173–174.

78. Michael V. Hazel, "The Dallas Public Library: Opening the Doors to the World of Books," *Heritage News*, XI (Fall, 1986), 15–18.

79. Michael V. Hazel, "Art for the People: Dallas' First Public Gallery," *Heritage News*, IX (Fall, 1984), 4–8.

80. This mixture is reflected in the city directories of the period and in the Sanborn Fire Insurance Maps for Dallas.

81. McDonald, *Dallas Rediscovered*, 103–104.

82. Ibid., 204, 211; promotional pamphlet for Oak Cliff in the collections of the Dallas Historical Society; Sam Acheson, *Dallas Yesterday* (Dallas: Southern Methodist University Press, 1977), 52–56.

83. McDonald, *Dallas Rediscovered*, 155–164.

84. Mohl, *The New City*, 38.

85. Dallas *Morning News*, Jan. 2, 1902.

86. Mohl, *The New City*, 118–119; Darwin Payne, *Big D* (Dallas: Three Forks Press, 1994), 8–19.

87. For a vivid description of the flood, see Payne, *Big D*, 19–26.

88. William H. Wilson, *The City Beautiful Movement* (Baltimore: Johns Hopkins University Press, 1989), 254–256.

89. For removal of the Pacific Avenue tracks, see William H. Wilson, "'Merely Unpractical Dreams,'" *Legacies*, II (Fall, 1990), 26–34.

90. For the Trinity levee project, see Jackie McElhaney, "Navigating the Trinity," in *Dallas Reconsidered*, ed. Michael V. Hazel (Dallas: Three Forks Press, 1995), 53–54.

91. For a synopsis of Dallas city plans from 1911 to 1995, see Chris Kelley, "Developing Dallas," Dallas *Morning News*, Apr. 21, 1996, 10J.

92. Payne, *Big D*, 49–53.

93. Mary Martha Thomas Hosford, *Southern Methodist University: Founding and Early Years* (Dallas: Southern Methodist University Press, 1955); Marshall Terry, "*From High on the Hilltop* . . ." (Dallas: Southern Methodist University Press, 1993).

94. Holmes and Saxon (eds.), *The WPA Dallas Guide*, 94.

95. For an excellent account of the KKK in Dallas, see Payne, *Big D*, 73–96.

96. Acheson, *35,000 Days in Texas*, 275–280; Darwin Payne, "*The Dallas Morning News* and the Ku Klux Klan," *Legacies*, IX (Spring, 1997), 16–27.

97. Payne. *Big D*, 96.

98. Ibid., 71–72.

99. J. H. Owens, writing in the Dallas *Gazette*, July 3, 1937, cited in Alan Govenor, "'Them Deep Ellum Blues,'" *Legacies*, II (Spring, 1990), 5.

100. Ibid., 6–8.

101. Rogers, *The Lusty Texans of Dallas*, 211–213, 246.

102. Acheson, *35,000 Days in Texas*, 273–274.

103. Holmes and Saxon (eds.), *The WPA Dallas Guide*, 210.

104. Dallas *Times Herald*, Sept. 28, 1927, cited in Payne, *Big D*, 121.

105. Payne, *Big D*, 115–117; Ryan Berube, "The Sky's the Limit," *Legacies*, VII (Spring, 1995), 32–37.

106. Holmes and Saxon (eds.), *The WPA Dallas Guide*, 96–97.

107. Robert Shelton, "Yankee Devils in Paradise?" *Legacies*, VI (Fall, 1994), 12–19.

108. James Howard, *Big D is for Dallas* (Austin: University Co-operative Society, 1957), 68, 77; H. Harold Wineburgh, *The Texas Banker: The Life and Times of Fred Farrel Florence* (Dallas: n.p., 1981), 126–135; David Nevin, *The Texans: What They Are—And Why* (New York: William Morrow and Co., 1968), 155–157; Payne, *Big D*, 144.

109. The other two principal banks were First National and Republic National.

110. Payne, *Big D*, 159–169.

111. In 1986, Fair Park was entered on the National Register of Historic Places as a national landmark. It contains the largest collection of 1930s Art Deco buildings in the country. Ron Tyler et al. (eds.), *New Handbook of Texas* (6 vols.; Austin: Texas State Historical Association, 1996), II, 937.

112. Kenneth Ragsdale, *The Year America Discovered Texas: Centennial '36* (College Station: Texas A&M University Press, 1987).

113. Payne, *Big D*, 170.

114. Ragsdale, *The Year America Discovered Texas*, 305.

115. Marvin Dulaney, "The Progressive Voters League," *Legacies*, III (Spring, 1991), 27–35.

116. Gwendolyn Rice, "Little Mexico and the Barrios of Dallas," *Legacies*, IV (Fall, 1992), 21–27.

117. Payne, *Big D*, 206.

118. Ibid., 172–173; Carol Estes Thometz, *The Decision Makers: The Power Structure of Dallas* (Dallas: Southern Methodist University Press, 1963), 57–58.

119. Robert B. Fairbanks, "The Good Government Machine: The Citizens Charter Association and Dallas Politics, 1930–1960," in *Essays on Sunbelt Cities*, ed. Robert B. Fairbanks and Kathleen Underwood (College Station: Texas A&M University Press, 1990), 125–150.

120. Dallas *Morning News*, Apr. 3, 1947, cited in Fairbanks, "Good Government Machine," 136–137.

121. Payne, *Big D*, 277.

122. Raymond A. Mohl, "The Transformation of Urban America since the Second World War," and Carl Abbott, "Sunbelt Cityscapes," in Fairbanks and Underwood (eds.), *Essays on Sunbelt Cities and Recent Urban America*.

123. Pam Lange and Mindie Lazarus-Black, *Family Business in Dallas: A Matter of Values* (Dallas: Dallas Public Library, 1982), 242.

124. Jim Schutze, *The Accommodation* (Secaucus, N.J.: Citadel Press, 1986); Payne, *Big D*, 256–259. Attempts to develop new residential neighborhoods for African Americans were consistently met with opposition. See William H. Wilson, "'This Negro Housing Matter,'" *Legacies*, VI (Fall, 1994), 28–40.

125. Dallas *Times Herald*, Dec. 3–9, 1951; Payne, *Big D*, 262; Schutze, *The Accommodation*, 72–73.

126. Glenn M. Linden, *Desegregating Schools in Dallas* (Dallas: Three Forks Press, 1995).

127. Payne, *Big D*, 297–302.

128. Ibid., 279–283.

129. Francine Carraro, *Jerry Bywaters: A Life in Art* (Austin: University of Texas Press, 1994), 172–204.

130. Payne, *Big D*, 285–286.

131. Ibid., 320.

132. Ibid., 321–322. SMU psychologist James Pennebaker conducted a survey that revealed that, following the assassination, coronary deaths, murders, and suicides all increased in Dallas. See Bill Minutaglio,"Quiet Healers," *Dallas Life* magazine, Dallas *Morning News*, Nov. 21, 1993.

133. Ibid., 323.

134. "*Look* and the National Municipal All-American Cities, 1970," *Look* (Mar. 23, 1971), 72–74, 76.

135. Interview with J. Erik Jonsson, Nov. 18, 1993; interview with Najeeb Hallaby, Jan. 13, 1994.

136. Payne, *Big D*, 333–335.

137. Ibid., 336–337.

138. Dallas *Times Herald*, Apr. 17, 1971, quoted ibid., 355.

139. Dallas *Morning News*, Nov. 25, 1974, quoted ibid., 359.

140. Payne, *Big D*, 362.

141. A 1987 study by James Pennebaker indicated that, twenty-five years after the assassination, approximately 70 percent of Dallas residents "think others still blame Dallas." See Minutaglio, "Quiet Healers."

142. Adlene Harrison had become Dallas's first woman mayor when she succeeded Wes Wise after he resigned to run for Congress. But Annette Strauss was the first woman actually elected to the position.

143. See maps published in the Dallas *Morning News*, Apr. 9, 1995, p. 45A.

144. Payne, *Big D*, 401.

Michael V. Hazel is a Dallas native who received his B.A. in history from Southern Methodist University and his M.A. and Ph.D. from the University of Chicago. He currently teaches Dallas history at SMU, serves as archivist for the A. H. Belo Corporation, and edits *Legacies*, a regional history journal.